C H U T E   C X O

Josh Holtzman
Professional EOS Implementer
310.709.9468 | josh@chutecxo.com

PRAISE FOR *TRACTION*

"The concepts and tools that have been masterfully captured in the pages of this book have provided some of the magic that has helped us grow our business 300% over the last five years. Don't miss it!"

CRAIG ERLICH
CEO, PULSE220

"The concepts in this book have changed my life! I'm now able to let go of the day to day, knowing I have developed a team that can efficiently handle the details. We have consistently grown every year for the last four years in a very tough market, while the competition has struggled."

RONALD A. BLANK
PRESIDENT, THE FRANKLIN COMPANIES

"Having coached and trained over 13,000 entrepreneurs, I know the challenges they face. This book is a must for any business owner and their management team. *Traction* provides a powerful, practical, and simple system for running your business."

DAN SULLIVAN
PRESIDENT AND FOUNDER, THE STRATEGIC COACH

"Prior to implementing the disciplines in this book my partner and I felt like we were running our business by the seat of our pants. With the *Traction* tools in place we now have faster growth, increased profitability and great people that we enjoy working with. Our growth rate has averaged over 20% per year. These results put us in a position to sell our company to a public company for above-normal multiples and reacquire the company after just a year and a half."

ROB DUBE
PRESIDENT, IMAGE ONE

"Gino's tools work. They really help us stay consistent and focused on our vision. The *Traction* principles have helped me build a solid leadership team, crystallize our plan, and create the discipline to take the organization to the next level."

SAM SIMON
PRESIDENT & CEO, ATLAS OIL COMPANY

"*Traction* is far and away the most potent and useful approach I've ever seen for running a successful company. The content is bulletproof! You have to read this book."

VINCE POSCENTE
AUTHOR OF *THE AGE OF SPEED*

"The content in *Traction* has improved my business and my life dramatically. I'm having more fun, and my sales and profits have increased by 50% over the past three years. The methodology keeps us on track, allows us to be creative, and helps us serve our clients better."

BOB SHENEFELT
CEO, RCS INTERNATIONAL

"The concepts in this book have revolutionized our enterprise. We are highly profitable, adroit, flexible, and have a results-oriented culture. Working with Gino's tools has made a meaningful difference in who we are today."

ALBERT M. BERRIZ
CEO, McKINLEY

"*Traction* is a must-read for the business owner/manager who desires a high performing business and a great quality of life. The concepts in this book have allowed me to not only maintain my focus on making my business the best it can be, but to also be the best family man I can be at the same time. *Traction* is like no other business book because it offers real, practical, easy-to-understand systems to run a business. Our company has experienced a powerful cultural shift."

DAN ISRAEL
PRESIDENT, ASPHALT SPECIALISTS, INC.

"This book will change your and your employees' lives. The tools are sensible, effective, and a must for any organization, entrepreneur, or leader. I personally use them within my national real estate valuation company and this year we grew 150%, after being in business for over 14 years."

DARTON CASE
PRESIDENT, THE ENTREPRENEURS' ORGANIZATION

"The concepts in *Traction* saved our company from mediocrity and propelled us to excellence. They have provided us with the tools to deal with any situation that might arise and better yet, to head off some situations at the pass. We now have all the right people in the right seats doing the right jobs. *Traction* has given me the confidence that we are moving forward as a company and as a team."

ROB TAMBLYN
PRESIDENT, THE BENEFITS COMPANY

"If you are an entrepreneur, leader or manager you must read this book. Together with my son and son-in-law, I was looking to rapidly grow the business that I had built over the last 35 years. The tools in this book were exactly what we needed to make that happen. By applying the *Traction* disciplines we have been able to grow revenue by 50% over the last three years and profit exponentially more."

ROBERT SCHECHTER, C.L.U., CH.F.C.
CHAIRMAN, SCHECHTER WEALTH STRATEGIES

"*Traction* is a must-read. What you will learn are the same tools that have enabled me to grow my business 100% over the last three years while staying balanced and having fun. This book will change your life."

BERNIE RONNISCH
PRESIDENT, RONNISCH CONSTRUCTION GROUP

"These tools have been an invaluable resource for Zoup! Our company has flourished, growing from five locations to just under 50 open and awarded. In addition to traction and accountability, these concepts have helped us create a strong, healthy, and skilled leadership team with clarity around the company's vision and each member's contribution to that vision. It has helped us clarify roles for the team and also for franchisees."

ERIC ERSHER
FOUNDER & CEO, ZOUP! FRESH SOUP COMPANY

"I had a well-run, profitable and growing business before we implemented the concepts in *Traction*. Today, a year after implementation, we have supercharged the business. We now have clarity of responsibilities and problem-solving frameworks, and the growth has been explosive even through the recession. Thank you for giving us the framework to really take off!"

BOB VERDUN
PRESIDENT, COMPUTERIZED FACILITY INTEGRATION, LLC (CFI)

"A note of thanks for all you have done for our firm. When we began implementing these concepts, I was not happy, my health was failing, and my stress level was so high, I was ready to give up. Business wasn't fun anymore. My business owned me—I didn't own my business. At the time, I had 10 employees and was ready to take it back to five and just settle for where I was. To consider more growth just meant more stress and more frustrations. In the last year and a half of working with you, we now have 12 employees, and our revenue has gone up by almost 100 percent in two years! The best part is, I am not only happier again but also have more freedom of time. I now spend 50 percent of my year in Nashville with my two children, their spouses, and my two granddaughters. More income, and less time combined with happier employees = one happy business owner. Many, many, many thanks!"

CURT WHIPPLE
OWNER, C. CURTIS FINANCIAL

TRACTION

OTHER BOOKS BY GINO WICKMAN

Decide!
Get a Grip (with Mike Paton)
Rocket Fuel (with Mark C. Winters)
How to Be a Great Boss (with René Boer)

TRACTION

GET A GRIP ON YOUR BUSINESS

GINO WICKMAN

BenBella

Dallas, Texas

BenBella Books, Inc.
10440 N. Central Expressway, Suite 800
Dallas, TX 75231
www.benbellabooks.com
Send feedback to feedback@benbellabooks.com

Printed in the United States of America

20 19 18 17 16 15 14 13 12 11

Library of Congress Cataloging-in-Publication Data is available for this title.

ISBN 978-1-936661-84-8 (cloth)
ISBN 978-1-936661-83-1 (paperback)

Originally published in hardcover by EOS in 2007
First Trade paperback edition 2011

Editing by Erin Kelley
Proofreading by Michael Fedison and Cape Cod Compositors, Inc.
Indexing by WordCo Indexing Services, Inc.
Cover design by Faceout Studio
Text design and composition by Neuwirth & Associates, Inc.
Supplemental interior changes by PerfecType, Nashville, TN
Printed by Lake Book Manufacturing

Distributed by Perseus Distribution
(www.perseusdistribution.com)

To place orders through Perseus Distribution:
Tel: 800-343-4499
Fax: 800-351-5073
E-mail: orderentry@perseusbooks.com

Special discounts for bulk sales (minimum of 25 copies) are available.
Please contact Aida Herrera at aida@benbellabooks.com.

To my dad, Floyd Wickman, one of the world's greatest entrepreneurs. This book would not exist without your teaching and mentoring.
It is a tribute to who you are.

And also to my wife, Kathy, my daughter, Alexis, and my son, Gino:
I am so proud, and I love each of you with all of my heart.

CONTENTS

INTRODUCTION

Humor me for a moment and mentally detach yourself from your day-to-day details. Forget all your pre-existing beliefs about how to run your organization. Now imagine a bird's-eye view of your business and look down on it from above. What do you see?

You're reading this book because you want your organization to be solid and well-run. You've already achieved a certain degree of success, and now you're ready for the next level. However, with this challenge comes a new set of obstacles; sheer will and brute force are no longer enough to survive. The question you're facing now is a new one: How can you elevate yourself to a position of true leadership?

What if I told you that by reading this book and applying its core principles, you could eliminate all of your business-related frustrations? That you could have great employees at all levels who share your vision, communicate with each other, solve their own problems, and demonstrate accountability? That your organization could not only run seamlessly, but also have the potential to scale up as large as you see fit?

I am telling you that, and you can. Believe it or not, you already have everything you need to make those changes. Put this system to work and you will accomplish all of the above, just as businesses across many different industries have been doing for years.

This book is not another silver bullet management book or flavor-of-the-month strategy. It contains no theory. It's based on real-world experience, practical wisdom, and timeless truths. More importantly, it works. Through hands-on experience, I have developed a practical but thorough method to help strengthen and reenergize your business.

If you're like most entrepreneurs, you're probably experiencing one or more of five common frustrations:

1. Lack of control: You don't have enough control over your time, the market, or your company. Instead of controlling the business, the business is controlling you.

2. People: You're frustrated with your employees, customers, vendors, or partners. They don't seem to listen, understand you, or follow through with their actions. You're not all on the same page.

3. Profit: Simply put, there's not enough of it.

4. The ceiling: Your growth has stopped. No matter what you do, you can't seem to break through and get to the next level. You feel overwhelmed and unsure of what to do next.

5. Nothing's working: You've tried various strategies and quick-fix remedies. None have worked for long, and as a result, your staff has become numb to new initiatives. You're spinning your wheels, and you need traction to move again.

Granted, a small minority of entrepreneurs and business owners do not suffer from these frustrations. They run their businesses using core disciplines that arrange the many moving parts of their organization into a well-oiled machine. Some of these owners are naturals who don't even realize they're doing anything special. Most of us, though, aren't so lucky.

What I teach business leaders is simple, but not simplistic. I help them melt away the five common frustrations by implementing the same basic tools that those successful organizations employ. As a result, business leaders come out feeling more in control, happier, and less stressed. Their organizations are more profitable, more focused, and staffed by great employees.

You are not your business. Your business is an entity in and of itself. Yes, you created it, but in order to find success, you have to turn it into a self-sustaining organism. Reaching the next level requires more than just a product or service, or a simple determination to succeed. You need skills, tools, and a system to optimize your people, processes, execution, management, and communication. You need strong guiding principles that will work for your company day in and day out.

This book contains all the tools and components that make up the Entrepreneurial Operating System (EOS). EOS is a holistic, self-sustaining system that addresses the six aspects of your business. Master the individual elements of EOS and you'll be able to integrate them into a powerful framework that will help you gain traction and realize the vision you've always had for your company.

This operating system didn't hit me like a lightning bolt; I've been refining it in the real world for over 20 years. It came through countless real-world hands-on experiences one lesson at a time. My journey has been a quest to understand what makes great entrepreneurs and businesses so successful. Through turning around and then selling my own family's business, my involvement in The Entrepreneurs' Organization, and learning from my many amazing mentors, I've been blessed with many experiences, challenges, and lessons. In the last 11 years alone, I've completed more than 1,300 full-day sessions with the leadership teams of over 120 entrepreneurial organizations. That adds up to over 10,000 hours of hands-on planning, teaching, coaching, facilitating, and solving leadership problems; EOS is the culmination of all that hard work.

My typical client is an entrepreneurial small to mid-size organization ($2 million to $50 million in revenue with 10 to 250 employees), growth-oriented, willing to change, and willing to be vulnerable (as in being open-minded, willing to admit weaknesses, and willing to face reality). If that describes you, you're starting with everything you need. You will not have to master an endless stream of new techniques. Instead, you'll learn what successful organizations do to run a frustration-free business and gain renewed energy, focus, and excitement for your business. Join me on this journey to better control your business and bust through the ceiling—to have better balance, better results, more fun, and more profitability.

At this very moment, people who follow The EOS Process are out there running very successful businesses. On average, my clients' businesses grow revenue by 18 percent per year. In addition, unlike many theoretical authors, I too am out there somewhere, working with a leadership team hands-on and applying, testing, and proving these tools. I am an entrepreneur like you and have been since I was 21 years old. This is not management theory. EOS is working every day.

Be careful what you wish for—with this system, you'll get it. After EOS, you'll make quicker decisions to change people, strategy, systems, and processes where necessary. It will help you reduce needless complexity, identify and remove distractions, identify and troubleshoot any problems, and keep you and your people engaged and focused on a single vision.

The Six Key Components of the Entrepreneurial Operating System (EOS) go right to the roots of the six most important aspects of your business and strengthen them, eliminating all of your symptomatic issues by solving the real ones. EOS is a method—even a way of life—that will help you crystallize your vision and build a strong organization. By first understanding and then implementing what you learn, you will be able to accurately monitor the pulse of your company and know how it's really doing.

At some point on this journey, you're likely to say, as every client does, "Hey, this stuff is simple." That's because it is. If you're looking for the next fashionable MBA methodology, this isn't it. EOS consists of timeless, practical, universal principles that have been tested in almost every kind of organization. What's dramatically new is the integration of these best practices into a complete system for organizing and operating your business that will endure for decades to come.

I have tremendous respect for you, the entrepreneur. You take risks, you drive the economy, you keep your country at the forefront of innovation, and you sacrifice everything to fulfill your dreams. As a result, you create most of the jobs and give other people the opportunities to live their dreams. My passion and purpose is to help you succeed. Now, let's begin this journey at the end by envisioning what your company could look like after implementing EOS.

Before we begin, I'm proud to add this new final paragraph to the introduction of this expanded edition of *Traction*. With its success and five more years of real-world experiences under my belt, I've updated this book to include a new chapter intended to help you, the reader, implement these tools more purely. In many places, I've added clearly marked sidebars, which include additional teachings and new discoveries made over the last five years, and I've added over 50 updates throughout the book. Please enjoy this second edition of *Traction*, and if at any time you get stuck, don't hesitate to reach out to us, as we now have a complete online support platform to help the many thousands of leaders in our community at no cost.

CHAPTER 1

THE ENTREPRENEURIAL
OPERATING SYSTEM

STRENGTHENING THE SIX
KEY COMPONENTS

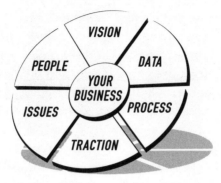

E very great system is made up of a core group of basic components. The same applies to a business. The Entrepreneurial Operating System (EOS) identifies Six Key Components of any organization. In the words of an EOS client, "I used to worry about 100 different things. Once I learned there were six components to my business and I focused on only those, those 100 different things I'd been worrying about went away. EOS made running the business simpler."

You're probably worrying needlessly about a hundred different things yourself. Let's try to remove you from some of those worries by taking a wide-angle view of your business and its components. Below are the Six Key Components of any organization.

VISION

Successful business owners not only have compelling visions for their organizations, but also know how to communicate those visions to the people around them. They get everyone in the organization seeing the same clear image of where the business is going and how it's going to get there. It sounds easy, but it's not.

Are your staff all rowing in the same direction? Chances are they're not. Some are rowing to the right, some are rowing to the left, and some probably aren't rowing at all. If you met individually with each of your employees and asked them what the company's vision was, you'd likely get a range of different answers.

The more clearly everyone can see your vision, the likelier you are to achieve it. Focus everyone's energy toward one thing and amazing results will follow. In his book *Focus*, Al Ries illustrates the point in this way: The sun provides the earth with billions of kilowatts of energy, yet if you stand in it for an hour, the worst you will get is a little sunburn. On the other hand, a few watts of energy focused in one direction is all a laser beam needs to cut through diamonds.

In the Vision Component chapter, you will use a tool called The Vision/Traction Organizer (V/TO) to focus your people on one target and become like that laser beam. The tool simplifies strategic planning by distilling your vision into simple points that allow you to clearly define who you are as an organization, where you're going and how you'll get there. It will help you define your sweet spot as an organization and keep you focused on the areas in which you excel most. It will also define your marketing strategy and crystallize your 10-year target, three-year picture, and one-year plan. In addition, you'll learn to effectively convey your vision to your staff and ensure that it's embraced by everyone.

PEOPLE

Successful leaders surround themselves with great people. You can't build a great company without help. EOS cuts through buzzwords such as "A players," "platinum," "100 percenters," and "superstars" to provide a practical understanding of the two essential ingredients of any great team: the *right people* in the *right seats*.

Be truly honest with yourself. Are all of your people the right ones for their jobs? The reality is that some are probably hurting your cause more than helping. The People Analyzer tool in Chapter 4 will help identify the right people by teaching you how to determine who shares your core values. It will also teach you to simplify how you hire, fire, review, reward, and recognize people in your organization.

This process will prompt you to step back and look at your overall structure. You'll ask yourself hard questions about the way your business is organized. You'll also learn the power of the Accountability Chart, as well as how to structure your company the right way while clearly defining the roles and responsibilities within your organization.

Once you have the right structure in place, you'll be able to focus on putting the right people in the right seats. There will be no gray area when you incorporate the next tool, GWC, which addresses the three absolutes for any good hire. They must *get it*, *want it*, and have the *capacity* to do it. Once you incorporate GWC into The People Analyzer, you'll have a working tool that determines which people are the right ones and which people are in the right seats.

DATA

The best leaders rely on a handful of metrics to help manage their businesses. The Data Component frees you from the quagmire of managing personalities, egos, subjective issues, emotions, and intangibles by teaching you which metrics to focus on.

My business mentor, Sam Cupp, owned several companies totaling over $300 million in sales, including QEK Global Solutions, a worldwide fleet management company that he built into a $100-million business and then sold. He is one of the best businessmen I've ever met. I was blessed to have him take me under his wing at a young age and teach me everything he knew. Of all of that wisdom, the most useful thing he taught me was the power of managing my business through a Scorecard.

A Scorecard is a weekly report containing five to 15 high-level numbers for the organization. In the Data Component chapter, you will learn to create and implement this powerful tool into your company. It will enable you to have a pulse of your business on a weekly basis, predict future developments, and quickly identify when things have fallen off the track. Because you're regularly reviewing the numbers, you'll be able to quickly spot and solve problems as they come up as opposed to reacting to bad numbers in a financial statement long after the fact.

A Scorecard allows you to monitor your business no matter where you are. You won't have to suffer from the uneasy feeling of not quite knowing what's going on in your business, nor will you have to waste time asking a half dozen people for the real story. The answers will be right at your fingertips.

In addition to learning to create and implement your Scorecard, you will take your data management to the next level by learning to empower each person in your organization. Everyone will have a clear, meaningful, and manageable number that he or she is accountable for on a regular basis.

ISSUES

Issues are the obstacles that must be faced to execute your vision. Just as an individual's success is directly proportionate to his or her ability to solve any issues that arise, the same holds true for a company.

One helpful by-product of strengthening the first three EOS components is transparency. Execute them properly and you will have created an open organization where there is nowhere to hide. As a result, you will smoke out issues that have been holding you back.

The good news is that, in the history of business, there has only ever been a handful of different kinds of issues. The same ones come up over and over again. In time, you will become an expert at identifying them and knocking them down. To the degree you can identify them, discuss them honestly in a healthy environment, and learn to eradicate them, you will achieve your vision.

Regardless of how long you've been plagued by your problems, the Issues Component represents a huge opportunity. In the bustle of day-to-day operations, most companies don't invest the time required to adequately solve their issues. The irony is that by taking the time to address a problem, you will save two to 10 times that amount of time in the future.

In the Issues Component chapter, you will learn how to use the Issues List at all levels in your organization, allowing you to compartmentalize and prioritize all issues. In addition, you'll benefit by creating an open and honest culture where people feel safe to speak the truth and voice their concerns. You will then use the Issues Solving Track to eradicate these issues. This powerful tool is an efficient way to identify, discuss, and solve your organizational issues in a lasting and meaningful way.

By the end of the Issues Component chapter, you and your staff should understand how to identify various issues, create and manage an Issues List, and master the Issues Solving Track, taking you one step closer to building a problem-solving work environment.

PROCESS

Your processes are your *Way* of doing business. Successful organizations see their *Way* clearly and constantly refine it. Due to lack of knowledge, this secret ingredient in business is the most neglected of the Six Key Components. Most entrepreneurs don't understand how powerful process can be, but when you apply it correctly, it works like magic, resulting in simplicity, scalability, efficiency, and profitability.

You will not get your company to the next level by keeping your processes in your head and winging it as you go. Ask yourself: Have you documented the way you want everything done in your organization? Do your people know what processes they are following and why? Are they all executing the required procedures uniformly? Are they skipping steps? By deciding what the process is and training everyone to follow it, you will enhance your troubleshooting abilities, reduce your errors, improve efficiency, and increase your bottom line.

In the Process Component chapter, we will identify, address, and document each of your core processes using the Three-Step Process Documenter. This tool will help you crystallize your business model by capturing the blueprint for the machine you aspire to build in a single document. From there, you will learn how to get your staff to understand the value of these processes and begin to follow them.

By the end of the journey, your processes will be clearly identified, documented, understood, and followed by everyone in your organization.

TRACTION

In the end, the most successful business leaders are the ones with traction. They execute well, and they know how to bring focus, accountability, and discipline to their organization.

Due to fear and lack of discipline, the Traction Component is typically most organizations' weakest link. The inability to make a business vision a reality is epidemic. Consider it a new take on an old quote: Vision without traction is merely hallucination. All over the world, business consultants frequently conduct multiple-day strategic planning sessions and charge tens of thousands of dollars for teaching what is theoretically great material. The downside is that after making you feel warm and fuzzy about your direction, these same consultants rarely teach how to bring your vision down to the ground and make it work in the real world.

How would you rate the accountability throughout your organization on a scale of 1 to 10? Most new clients that start The EOS Process rate their accountability somewhere around 4. Gaining traction requires two disciplines. First, everyone in the organization should have Rocks, which are clear 90-day priorities designed to keep them focused on what is most important. The second discipline requires implementing what is called a Meeting Pulse at all levels in the organization, which will keep everyone focused, aligned, and in communication.

In the Traction Component chapter, you will first learn how to set Rocks so that everyone will know what they are accountable for in the coming 90 days. Next, you'll learn how to implement a Meeting Pulse. While most people feel that meetings are a waste of time, they are necessary and useful tools. As part of the component, you'll learn how to make meetings enjoyable, productive, and worthwhile. The Level 10 Meeting Agenda is a tool that will help you get to the core of what makes for great meetings, namely conflict and resolution.

By the end of Chapter 8, everyone in your organization should know how to establish and achieve their Rocks. They'll also be engaging in effective, productive meetings using the tried and true Level 10 Meeting Agenda.

Now that we know what the Six Key Components are, we need to assess where your company is right now. The Organizational Checkup at the end of this chapter will tell you exactly where you are on this path. You can also fill out the questionnaire online at **www.eosworldwide.com /checkup**. Several of the terms won't be clear to you yet, but in a short time you'll know exactly what they mean. Fill out the questionnaire and use the attached key to get your results.

You'll be coming back to this checkup on a routine basis. The goal is to make progress every 90 days. Each time you fill out the checkup, your overall percentage should increase. It's unreasonable to think that you'll jump from 20 percent to 80 percent overnight, but you will make steady progress.

In summary, successful businesses operate with a crystal clear vision that is shared by everyone. They have the right people in the right seats. They have a pulse on their operations by watching and managing a handful of numbers on a weekly basis. They identify and solve issues promptly in an open and honest environment. They document their processes and ensure that they are followed by everyone. They establish priorities for each employee and ensure that a high level of trust, communication, and accountability exists on each team.

The Six Key Components together make up The EOS Model. Most organizations operate below 50 percent. If they succeed, it's in spite of themselves. Although it's nearly impossible to reach 100 percent in every component, achieving over 80 percent will turn your company into a well-oiled machine. All the things you've been worrying about will simply fall into place, and the common frustrations that have been plaguing you will go away.

Now that the big picture is clear, let's begin the journey. But before we dive headfirst into the nuts and bolts of the first component, you'll have to free yourself from the bad habits and unhealthy practices that are holding you back. This is called letting go of the vine.

ORGANIZATIONAL CHECKUP

For each statement below, rank your business on a scale of 1 to 5 where 1 is weak and 5 is strong.

                           1 2 3 4 5

1. We have a clear vision in writing that has been properly communicated and is shared by everyone.

2. Our core values are clear, and we are hiring, reviewing, rewarding, and firing around them.

3. Our core business is clear, and our systems and processes reflect that.

4. Our 10-year target is clear and has been communicated to everyone.

5. Our target market is clear, and our sales and marketing efforts are focused on it.

6. Our differentiators are clear, and all of our sales and marketing efforts communicate them.

7. We have a proven process for doing business with our customers. It has been named and visually illustrated, and everyone is adhering to it.

8. All of the people in our organization are the right people.

9. Our accountability chart (organizational chart of roles and responsibilities) is clear, complete, and constantly updated.

10. Everyone is in the right seat.

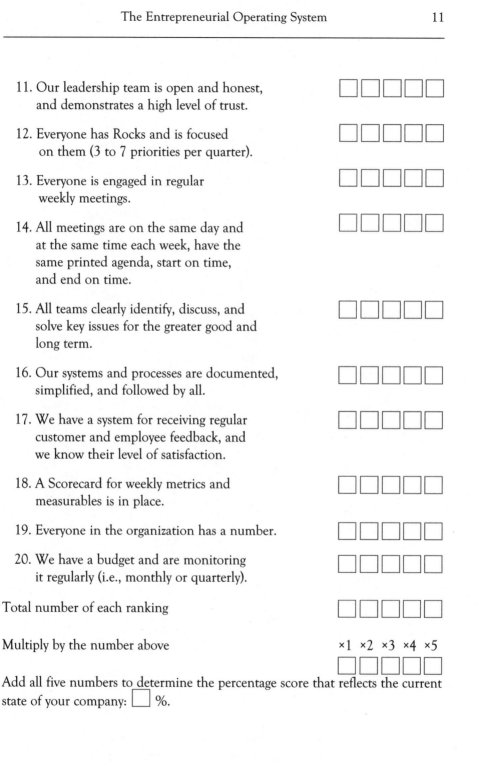

11. Our leadership team is open and honest, and demonstrates a high level of trust. ☐☐☐☐☐

12. Everyone has Rocks and is focused on them (3 to 7 priorities per quarter). ☐☐☐☐☐

13. Everyone is engaged in regular weekly meetings. ☐☐☐☐☐

14. All meetings are on the same day and at the same time each week, have the same printed agenda, start on time, and end on time. ☐☐☐☐☐

15. All teams clearly identify, discuss, and solve key issues for the greater good and long term. ☐☐☐☐☐

16. Our systems and processes are documented, simplified, and followed by all. ☐☐☐☐☐

17. We have a system for receiving regular customer and employee feedback, and we know their level of satisfaction. ☐☐☐☐☐

18. A Scorecard for weekly metrics and measurables is in place. ☐☐☐☐☐

19. Everyone in the organization has a number. ☐☐☐☐☐

20. We have a budget and are monitoring it regularly (i.e., monthly or quarterly). ☐☐☐☐☐

Total number of each ranking ☐☐☐☐☐

Multiply by the number above ×1 ×2 ×3 ×4 ×5
☐☐☐☐☐

Add all five numbers to determine the percentage score that reflects the current state of your company: ☐ %.

SCORING RESULTS

If your score falls between:

20 and **34**%	Please read on. This book will change your life.
35 and **49**%	You are normal. But would you prefer normal or great?
50 and **64**%	You are above average, but there is still room for improvement.
65 and **79**%	You are well above average.
80 and **100**%	This is where most EOS clients end up. This is your goal.

CHAPTER 2

LETTING GO
OF THE VINE

An entrepreneur slips and falls off the edge of a cliff. On his way down, he manages to grab onto the end of a vine. He's hanging there, a thousand feet from the top and a thousand feet from the bottom. His situation seems hopeless, so he looks up to the clouds, and decides, for the first time, to pray. "Is anybody up there?" he asks. After a long silence, a deep voice bellows down from the clouds: *"Do you believe?"* "Yes," replies the entrepreneur. *"Then let go of the vine,"* says the voice. The entrepreneur pauses for a second, looks up again, and finally responds, "Is there anybody else up there?"

Most business owners are unable to reach the next level because they are simply not ready to let go of the vine. You might know the feeling; you want to see your business grow, but at the same time, you're frustrated, tired, and unwilling to take on any more risk. The truth is that before you can grow, you'll need to take a leap of faith. But don't worry—you won't have to act until you are comfortable and clear on all of the EOS tools.

Here's a textbook example of the man hanging from the vine. He'd only started The EOS Process because his head of sales and marketing had begged him to. At the time, this man had his hands in every aspect of the business. His makeshift leadership team was a sham because he pulled all the strings. On top of that, he was logging 80 work hours a week and was overworked to the point that he'd actually started to nod off during meetings. He was a zombie.

But once, in an uncharacteristic moment of vulnerability, he admitted to me in confidence that he didn't want to live that way any longer. He put his faith in The EOS Process, and in two years he managed to elevate himself to a true leader for an organization that had a solid leadership team in place. Now, he spends more time with his family, he's decidedly less stressed, and he's generating more profit than ever.

If you're not happy with the current state of your company, you have three choices. You can live with it, leave it, or change it. If the first two are not an option, it's time to admit that you don't want to live this way any longer.

Change is scary. You're not alone in feeling anxious about jeopardizing what you already have. But despite these worries, it's time for a shift in thinking. You need to change from believing that you are your company and letting it become its own entity. With the right vision, structure, and people in place, your company can evolve and realize its full potential. To be truly ready for this change, you must be willing to embrace the following four fundamental beliefs:

1. You must build and maintain a true leadership team.

2. Hitting the ceiling is inevitable.

3. You can only run your business on one operating system.

4. You must be open-minded, growth-oriented, and vulnerable.

BUILDING A TRUE LEADERSHIP TEAM

Would you prefer a dictatorship or a true leadership team approach to running your business? Both leadership methods can work, so you have to decide. The philosophy of this book advocates a healthy leadership team approach, where you build a team of people that define the company's vision with you. These leaders all have clear accountabilities and must be able to take initiative over their respective departments. You must also all remain open and honest about all issues and be willing to fight for what is best for the company as a whole.

Dictatorships not only are exhausting, but also preclude future growth. It's simple math. One person can only make so many decisions and solve so many problems. You cannot build an enduring, successful organization that lives beyond you if your organization is designed to crumble the minute you step aside.

Until now, you've probably been holding all the pieces together on your own. But once your organization reaches a certain size, you won't be able to lead that way. If you want to grow, it's not possible to maintain a hand in sales, service, accounting, complaints, and follow-up on a regular basis.

This means that it's time to let others take control of those areas, and that you have to decide who you want to do so. Each of your departmental heads should be better than you in his or her respective position. Of course, you will need to give them clear expectations and instill a system for effective communication and accountability. Once you have the right people in the right seats, let them run with it.

Your job right now is to select these people wisely. If they don't already work in your organization, you'll have to find them elsewhere. Best-selling author and highly sought-after speaker Patrick Lencioni summarizes this very point in his book *Obsessions of an Extraordinary Executive: The Four Disciplines at the Heart of Making Any Organization World Class*. His first rule of building a healthy organization: "Build and maintain a cohesive leadership team."

Once your team is in place, each member needs to agree that the problems in the organization are also his or her responsibility. Once you take responsibility for a problem, you can help to solve it. Don't worry if you don't know how to solve a particular problem just yet—that will all be covered by the Issues Solving Track in Chapter 6.

The next leap of faith you have to take is this: As goes the leadership team, so goes the company. Your leadership team must present a united front to the rest of your organization. In a nuclear family, when the child doesn't like the answer from Mom, he or she might go to Dad. In your company, there can be only one answer, and your leadership team needs to parent everyone to greatness.

HITTING THE CEILING IS INEVITABLE

Organizations usually expand in spurts, by smashing through a series of ceilings. Reaching the natural limits of your existing resources is a by-product of growth, and a company continually needs to adjust its existing state if it hopes to expand through the next ceiling. You and your leadership team need to understand this, because you will hit the ceiling on three different levels: as an organization, departmentally, and as individuals.

In all of these instances, growth is your only option. If you're not growing, be it internally or externally, you're dying. Most companies strive for external growth, but internal growth also leads to future greatness. In fact, most companies *need* to start with a focus on internal growth before they can even think about external growth. The paradox is that they will actually grow faster externally in the long run if they are focused internally from the outset.

Schechter Wealth Strategies (SWS) exemplifies this point. Founded by Robert Schechter in 1971, SWS built a solid organization with a great reputation. After being joined by his son Marc and his son-in-law Jason Zimmerman, Schechter decided to aggressively grow the company. Unfortunately, their internal operations were already at capacity, chaotic, and in need of reorganizing before the company could hope to expand. With a powerhouse sales team, a strong culture, and great product offerings, their only barrier was operations capacity. They had hoped to get operations open for business within a few months. To meet this extremely aggressive timeline, they needed to change their corporate structure, reassess their staff, and make their processes consistent.

Through hard work, focus, and determination, they eventually achieved this goal. They clarified their vision, set up the right structure, put great people in place, and streamlined their processes. After a little more than a year, their reorganization was finally open for business. That may seem like a large time investment, but it couldn't have happened any faster, and the results now speak for themselves. Thanks to their very talented team, they have grown an average of 50 percent per year for the last three years. In the long run, they have grown faster than if they had started aggressively selling and forced the new business into an operational structure that couldn't handle the increased sales. The entire structure might have imploded, causing them to upset and lose valuable customers. Instead, the patience and hard work they put in paid off. If your organization needs an internal transformation first, be honest with yourself and spend the next one or two years growing internally and honing your business model so it can support external revenue growth.

But regardless of whether you grow inside or out, you're going to hit the ceiling. While there are a lot of differing statistics out there on the subject, they all point to the same conclusion: Many organizations fail because they're unable to survive these growing pains. On its official website, the U.S. Small Business Administration purports that "roughly 50 percent of small businesses fail within the first five years." In a study published by the Monthly Labor Review in 2005, economist Amy E. Knaup states that 56 percent of businesses die within the first four years. And in his book *The E-Myth* and *The E-Myth Revisited*, author Michael Gerber paints an even scarier picture, saying that 80 percent of businesses fail in their first five years and 80 percent of those remaining will fail somewhere between years six through ten.

The good news is that you can survive hitting the ceiling by choosing a leadership team that possesses five core leadership abilities. Above all else, your leaders need to be able to simplify, delegate, predict, systemize, and structure. To the degree that you and your team apply these five abilities, you will grow to the next level. Let's take a look at them one by one.

SIMPLIFY

The acronym KISS ("keep it simple, stupid") is your mantra here. Simplifying your organization is key. This entails streamlining the rules you operate under as well as how they're communicated. The same goes for your processes, systems, messages, and vision. Most organizations are too complex when they begin. Use models, visuals, acronyms, and checklists to simplify processes and procedures, because as your organization grows, it will get more complex. Henry David Thoreau got to the core of the issue in *Walden*, but Ralph Waldo Emerson later did him one better:

> "Simplify, simplify." Henry David Thoreau
>
> "One 'simplify' would have sufficed." Ralph Waldo Emerson

Dan Sullivan, the creator of The Strategic Coach® Program, makes the point as follows: "No further progress and growth is possible for an organization until a new state of simplicity is created." With its many tools, the entire EOS process is designed to help you create that new state of simplicity. It's a common thread you'll see over and over again throughout this book: Less is more.

DELEGATE

Your ability to break through the ceiling also depends on your ability to delegate. Be prepared to "delegate and elevate" to your true god-given skill set. You'll have to delegate some of your responsibilities and elevate yourself to operate at your highest and best use. It's not practical for you to remain chef, head waiter, and dishwasher as your company grows. By hanging on to all the tiny details, you're actually constricting the company's growth. When you experience that personal growth, the company will grow under you. This is exactly what is meant by letting go of the vine.

When you let go, however, you need to make sure you're letting go of the right duties. The responsibilities that you delegate to other people have to be tasks that you have outgrown. These include things such as opening mail, writing proposals, approving invoices, and handling customer complaints. Sometimes we're afraid to pass off jobs that aren't much fun for others, but, at a certain point, you'll have to. The beauty of this transition is that there are people who have the skills and enthusiasm to do these jobs.

Not only will you need to learn how to delegate and elevate, but the people around you will as well. Just as you need to figure out how to build an extension of yourself, your team can also extend the company by building teams under them, thus ensuring the company's continued growth.

PREDICT

Prediction in business is done on two basic levels: Long-term and Short-term.

Long-term prediction. Publicly held companies predict earnings. When they later announce their actual earnings, either they hit the prediction or they don't. If they hit it, their stock continues to climb. If they miss, their stock simply drops. In a small to mid-size privately held organization, you don't have the luxury of missing your prediction. If you do, it may put you out of business.

Long-term predicting is the forecast of everything 90 days and beyond. To do so, your leadership team has to know where the organization is going and how you expect to get there. You do this by starting with the far future and working your way back. What is your 10-year target? What is your three-year picture? Your one-year plan? What do you have to accomplish in the next 90 days in order to be on track?

At first, this task may seem daunting, so let's take a little pressure off. No one has a crystal ball. No one can know what will happen tomorrow with certainty. Long-term predicting is not really about foretelling what will happen; it's making a decision about what you will do tomorrow based on what you know today.

Put another way, your leadership team has to "climb the tree" more often than others. I liken long-term prediction to a team of short-sighted people cutting a road through a jungle. They may be the most productive team that's ever cut a road, or they may be twice as productive as any other team before them. However, if there's no leader there to climb a tree and tell them where the road is going, they might very well be cutting a zigzag. Get good at taking the long view. As leaders, you'll need to stop working in the business 100 percent of the time, and as Michael Gerber, author of *The E-Myth* and *The E-Myth Revisited*, puts it, work *on* the business every so often instead. This discipline will get you to where you want to go faster.

Short-term prediction. While the long-term view addresses business needs 90 days and beyond, short-term focuses on the immediate future. These are the issues that will arise on a daily or weekly basis, and your ability to solve them will affect the long-term greater good of the organization.

As a leader in an organization, you're probably hit with at least half a dozen problems a day. Most leaders are so buried in the day-to-day grind that they'll typically think up flimsy workarounds just to get nagging issues out of their way so they can make it to the next week. If this happens long enough, their whole organization will come to be held together by duct tape and twine, and it will ultimately implode. You'll need to do a good job of predicting so that you can make those problems go away forever and avoid a similar fate.

SYSTEMIZE

There was probably a time when your business demanded that you fly by the seat of your pants. This involved reacting to every customer request, thinking on your toes, and being creative on the fly. At some point, though, certain actions have revealed themselves as redundant. That's when you should systemize them.

There are really only a handful of core processes that make any organization function. Systemizing involves clearly identifying what those core processes are and integrating them into a fully functioning machine. You will have a human resource process, a marketing process, a sales process, an operating process, a customer-retention process, an accounting process, and so on. These must all work together in harmony, and the methods you use should be crystal clear to everyone at all levels of the organization.

The first step is to agree as a leadership team on what these processes are and then to give them a name. This is your company's *Way* of doing business. Once you all agree on your *Way*, you will simplify, apply technology to, document, and fine-tune these core processes. In doing so, you will realize tremendous efficiencies, eliminate mistakes, and make it easier for managers to manage and for you to increase your profitability.

By systemizing your organization, you will start to see how all five leadership abilities work together to break through the ceiling. There is a direct correlation between organizational adherence to core processes and your own ability to let go. Handing over a turnkey system to an accountable leader makes it easier for you to delegate and elevate. As long as he or she follows the process and possesses the skill set to do the job, you'll be confident that the job at hand will be accomplished correctly.

STRUCTURE
Lastly, you and your leadership team will need to structure your organization correctly. Your company needs to be organized in a way that reduces complexity and creates accountability. In addition, this structure should also be designed to boost you to the next level. Too many organizations become stuck because they are set in their old ways and unwilling to change to fit their expansion.

Unfortunately, the structures of most small companies are either too loose or non-existent. Many of them have structures governed by ego, personality, and fear. You'll learn how to use the Accountability Chart so that you don't fall into this trap. This will enable you to implement a structure that encourages expansion and clearly defines everyone's roles and responsibilities.

In summary, once you understand that hitting the ceiling is inevitable, you and your leadership team must employ these five leadership abilities to reach the next level: (1) simplify the organization, (2) delegate and elevate, (3) predict both long-term and short-term, (4) systemize, and (5) structure your company the right way. The tools you're about to learn are all designed specifically to help you acquire those abilities.

YOU CAN ONLY RUN YOUR BUSINESS ON ONE OPERATING SYSTEM

You must have one abiding vision, one voice, one culture, and one operating system. This includes a uniform approach to how you meet, how you set priorities, how you plan and set your vision, the terminology you use, and the way you communicate with employees. EOS is an operating system that puts everybody on the same page. Just as a computer program is made up of components that organize activity and various data into a system that enables its users to be more productive, EOS does the same for a business.

If you assessed a handful of talented entrepreneurs, CEOs, sales managers, marketing directors, operations people, and finance people on leadership teams solely as individuals, you'd probably bet on their company being a success. But even talented leaders can't be effective without first settling on a single operating system for their company.

Often two talented people can speak two completely different languages:

"What are your objectives?" "You mean my goals?"

"What is the process?" "You mean the procedure?"

"No, that's a system."

"I prefer to set monthly objectives." "We've always set them weekly, and we call them action items."

Imagine coaching a sports team with two distinct methods or running a country with two governments. When systems work at cross purposes, your company is the ultimate loser. You cannot build a great organization on multiple operating systems—you must choose one. This book is offering you EOS.

YOU MUST BE OPEN-MINDED, GROWTH-ORIENTED, AND VULNERABLE

The late Dr. David Viscott, author of *Risking*, wrote, "If you cannot risk, you cannot grow. If you cannot grow, you cannot become your best. If you cannot become your best, you cannot be happy. If you cannot be happy, what else matters?"

Similarly, in your business environment, you have to be willing to be open to new and different ideas. If you don't know something, you have to admit that you don't know. You have to be willing to ask for and receive help. Most of all, you have to know your strengths and weaknesses and let other people who are more skilled than you in a certain area take charge.

Hard experience taught me the value of this belief. After one particularly unsuccessful engagement, I reflected back on why The EOS Process did not work. It came down to a simple truth: The members of the leadership team weren't growth-oriented, either internally or externally, nor were they willing to be vulnerable or open-minded. We accomplished very little because it was a constant battle to make decisions and discuss difficult issues. As a result, we both ended up dissatisfied. I now look for these warning signs in initial interviews with potential new clients. In many cases, I'm forced to help clients understand why they are not ready for The EOS Process.

You cannot embark on this journey if you're not willing to be vulnerable. You have to let your guard down to see your organization for what it is. Eliminate the facade with your leadership team, and invite openness and honesty. The leader who feels he has to have all of the answers and can never be wrong is completely missing the point. Being open-minded means being open to new ideas and being ready to change for the better. When your arms are folded, the wall is up and there is no getting in. The mind is like a parachute—it has to be open to work.

You must also be growth-oriented to take this journey. I have met many people who say they want to grow, only to discover after further questioning that they are petrified by the challenge and turbulence that growth creates. They are content at the size they are, and there are many good arguments in favor of contentment. EOS, however, is a system designed to help you grow.

In summary, the four fundamental beliefs are as follows:

1. You must build and maintain a true leadership team.

2. Hitting the ceiling is inevitable.

3. You can only run your business on one operating system.

4. You must be open-minded, growth-oriented, and vulnerable.

If you accept these beliefs, you're ready to let go of the vine. Now it's time to learn the tools that will help you rise to the next level and build a stronger organization. Over the course of the next six chapters, you will learn how to strengthen the Six Key Components of your organization. As you progress, you'll better understand the EOS structure, as well as why each component is reliant on the next. With that in mind, let's start where all traction starts: your vision.

CHAPTER 3

THE
VISION COMPONENT

DO THEY SEE
WHAT YOU ARE SAYING?

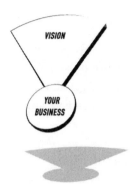

A few years ago, my dad made a humorous observation: People have a habit of firming up their convictions in conversation by asking the question, "Do you see what I'm saying?" On the surface, a question like that doesn't really make any sense—you really can't see what someone is *saying*. Later it dawned on me that the expression made all the sense in the world.

My dad is a visionary. He was my first mentor, and he taught me how to lead, manage, communicate, and deal with people, whether it be one or one thousand. He is one of only 140 Hall of Fame members of the National Speakers Association. He also built the number one real estate sales training company from the ground up and is a two-time finalist for the Ernst & Young Entrepreneur of the Year award.

As he well knows, most entrepreneurs can clearly see their vision. Their problem is that they make the mistake of thinking that everyone else in the organization sees it too. In most cases, they don't, and as a result, leaders end up frustrated, staff ends up confused, and great visions are left unrealized.

The process of gaining traction starts here. Clarify your vision and you will make better decisions about people, processes, finances, strategies, and customers.

Entrepreneurs must get their vision out of their heads and down onto paper. From there, they must share it with their organization so that everyone can see where the company is going and determine if they want to go there with you. By getting everyone on the same page, you will find that problems get solved more quickly. In *The Five Dysfunctions of a Team*, Patrick Lencioni credits a friend who built an organization from a start-up to a billion dollars in revenue with the following observation: "If you could get all the people in an organization rowing in the same direction, you could dominate any industry, in any market, against any competition, at any time."

A technology company that recently began The EOS Process came to me after hitting the ceiling for two straight years. The biggest problem was that the leadership team couldn't put its finger on why. There ended up being many reasons, but the key factor was that the company had no central vision. It was providing three very different services to the market, and because people had to change hats up to several times an hour to cater to different clients, the internal operations were needlessly complex.

With EOS, the company made the decision to focus in one direction. In two sessions, the leadership team clearly defined their vision of who they really were, what they really wanted to do, and where they really wanted to go. In a very short time, they simplified the organization and freed up resources by shedding two of its services. This allowed people to focus and excel in one area with one type of client. Now the company has clear goals and a laser-focused marketing strategy. Not surprisingly, it's once again beginning to grow. As a result of these decisions, it recently had its best first quarter ever, generating a 125 percent increase in revenue over the previous year's first quarter.

The first step is letting go because the vision you're about to clarify can't be about you. It has to define something bigger. You need to create a vision that points the way to a greater good. The sooner you do that, the sooner you will make better decisions that build an enduring company. To learn how to create a strong vision, you must first answer eight important questions.

ANSWERING THE EIGHT QUESTIONS

Let's start by dispelling the myth that a company's vision has to be a hundred pages long. You might need that level of detail for financing, but rarely is it necessary to build a great company. By simply answering eight questions, you and your leadership team should be able to clearly state your vision and ultimately enable everyone in the organization to "see" where you want to go.

The first tool in EOS is the Vision/Traction Organizer (V/TO). Not only is the V/TO designed to get your vision out of your head and onto paper, it will help you answer these eight questions. It's meant to help you create a clear picture of where the company is going and how it will get there. Most importantly, it does so simply, by boiling your vision down to only two pages. An example of a V/TO appears on the next page, and an electronic version of the V/TO can be downloaded free at **www.eosworldwide.com/vto.**

I first learned the power of simplicity in planning from my previous business partner, Ed Escobar. Along with my dad, Ed and I used to co-own and run a real estate sales training company. Once, Ed told me about the time prior to my joining the organization, when he had presented a quite lengthy business plan to my dad. After the first look, my dad said, "Can you condense it to 10 pages?" A little frustrated, Ed replied, "Sure." After some work he came back with a 10-page business plan. My dad liked it, but wondered aloud, "Could you condense it to two?" A little more perturbed, Ed complied once again. After some more work, the two-page business plan was created. When my dad's request to condense it to

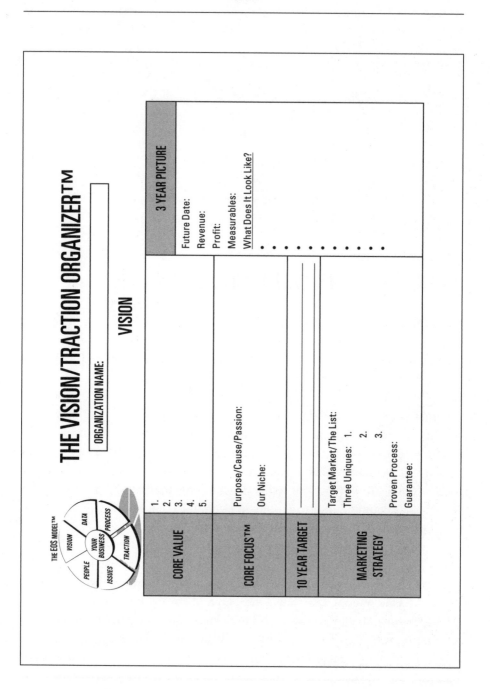

THE VISION/TRACTION ORGANIZER™

ORGANIZATION NAME:

VISION

CORE VALUE	1. 2. 3. 4. 5.
CORE FOCUS™	Purpose/Cause/Passion: Our Niche:
10 YEAR TARGET	
MARKETING STRATEGY	Target Market/The List: Three Uniques: 1. 2. 3. Proven Process: Guarantee:

3 YEAR PICTURE

Future Date:
Revenue:
Profit:
Measurables:
What Does It Look Like?
• • • • • • • • • • • •

THE EOS MODEL™
VISION — DATA — PROCESS
PEOPLE — YOUR BUSINESS — TRACTION
ISSUES

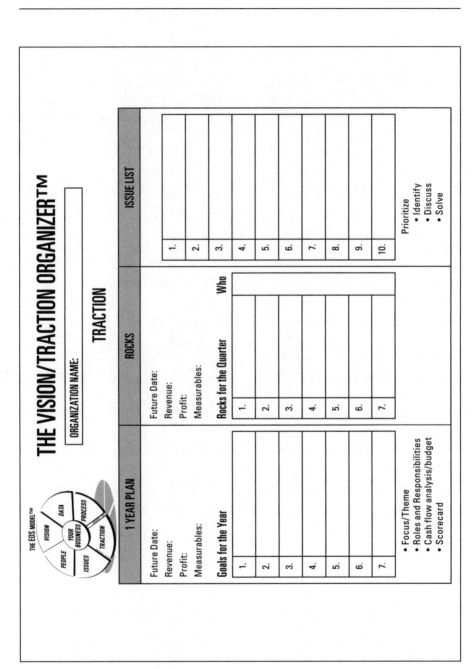

one page proved impossible, the idea of a two-page business plan was born. That simplistic business plan was the catalyst for the creation of the #1 real estate sales training company in North America. This led Ed to create a simplified business planning tool known as the Life Business Management Plan. It was the first tool I ever used for business planning.

That notion was eventually helped along by Verne Harnish. Author of *Mastering the Rockefeller Habits,* highly sought-after growth guru, founder of the Young Entrepreneurs' Organization (now the Entrepreneurs' Organization), and a regular contributor to *Fortune Small Business,* Harnish introduced me to his One-Page Strategic Plan, an additional inspiration for the V/TO.

In his book *The One Page Business Plan,* Jim Horan also deflates several popular myths, two of which are that "business plans must be long to be good" and that they take "six months, a significant amount of the owner's and key staff members' time, and expensive consultants" to create. As Horan understood, neither of these things is true. The simplified approach to strategic planning is generally the best approach.

What is vision? It's clearly defining who and what your organization is, where it's going and how it's going to get there. It should be simple to articulate your vision, because it's probably already in your head. Unfortunately, if there are five people on your leadership team, there may be five different variations of the company vision. The goal is to get you all on the same page. To the degree everyone on the team can answer the following eight questions and absolutely agree, you will have a clear vision.

By answering the following eight questions and filling out the V/TO, we will clarify exactly what your vision is. Let's get started. The eight questions are as follows:

1. What are your core values?
2. What is your core focus?
3. What is your 10-year target?
4. What is your marketing strategy?

5. What is your three-year picture?

6. What is your one-year plan?

7. What are your quarterly Rocks?

8. What are your issues?

Please note that it's recommended that you try to answer all eight questions in a full one- or two-day off-site session.

WHAT ARE YOUR CORE VALUES?

What are core values? They are a small set of vital and timeless guiding principles for your company. A good rule of thumb is to limit them to somewhere between three and seven. As always, less is more. These core values define your culture and who you truly are as people. When they are clear, you'll find they attract like-minded people to your organization. You will also find that when they are applied in your organization, they will weed out the people that don't fit. Once they're defined, you must hire, fire, review, reward, and recognize people based on these core values. This is how to build a thriving culture around them.

Unfortunately, most organizations have not defined their core values, and the resultant lack of clarity hinders their growth. When your people don't embrace your core values, their actions hurt your cause more than help it. By not defining what your values are, you have no way of knowing who believes in them and who doesn't.

When Image One started The EOS Process, the leadership team learned early on that we would be spending a few hours determining Image One's core values. Company co-owner Rob Dube argued that they must solve issues first. "We prepared a list of issues, and there are a ton," he said. "We should do this core-value thing after we solve those." In reply, I asked him to take a leap of faith and told him that if he didn't like the way our core-value search was going after an hour, we could move on to the list of issues. After the process was over, Rob changed his tune. "I didn't just like the way it was going, I loved it," he recalls. "I've been sold ever since. I tell that story to all new Image One team members and when I speak to groups about EOS. Defining core values changed our company, the way we do business, and the way we select our people."

Much has already been written on the power of identifying core values and instilling them in an organization. In the course of writing *Built to Last*, Jim Collins and Jerry I. Porras spent six years researching organizations that have endured through recessions and depressions for decades. One of their key findings was that in every case, these companies defined their core values in the very early stages and built a culture of people around them.

Despite that, the perceived value of core values has diminished as of late. After all the hype in the 1990s, they are now frequently regarded as clichéd and tired. This, ironically, is what makes them more vital than ever. In this book, they are the first step to forming your vision.

One important thing to understand is that core values already exist within your organization—they've just been lost in the day-to-day chaos. Your task is merely a matter of rediscovering what they are and instilling them as the rules you play by.

The following is the exact process all EOS clients follow for discovering their core values. First, schedule time with your leadership team. I recommend a minimum of two hours, preferably away from the office, as strategic thinking is always best done off-premises. In that meeting, you proceed as follows:

STEP 1
Have each member list three people who, if you could clone them, would lead you to market domination. These three names should preferably come from inside the organization. Once each person has his or her three, post all of the names on a whiteboard for everyone to see.

STEP 2
Go over the names and list the characteristics that those people embody. What are the qualities they exemplify? What do they do that puts them on the list? Start with a long list so that you can see all the possibilities. To help your thought process, here is a list of real-world core values:

- Unequivocal excellence
- Continually strives for perfection
- Wins

- Does the right thing
- Compassion
- Honesty and integrity
- Hungry for achievement
- Is enthusiastic, energetic, tenacious, and competitive
- Encourages individual ability and creativity
- Maintains accountability
- Services the customer above all else
- Works hard
- Is never satisfied
- Is interested in continuous self-improvement
- Helps first
- Exhibits professionalism
- Encourages individual initiative
- Growth-oriented
- Treats everyone with respect
- Provides opportunity based on merit;
  no one is entitled to anything
- Has creativity, dreams, and imagination
- Has personal integrity
- Isn't cynical
- Exhibits modesty and humility alongside confidence
- Practices fanatical attention to consistency and detail
- Is committed
- Understands the value of reputation
- Is fun
- Is fair
- Encourages teamwork

STEP 3

Your organization's core values are somewhere in that long list you've just created. Now, narrow it down. In your first edit, circle which ones are truly important, draw a line through the ones that are not, and combine those that are similar. Remember, the rule of thumb is between three and seven; after the first round, you should have the list down to somewhere between five and 15.

STEP 4

Here is where you're going to make some tough decisions. Through group discussion and debate, decide which values really belong and are truly core. Remember, your goal is to get your list down to between three and seven.

Here are some examples of EOS clients' real-world core values:

McKinley
- Can do
- Gumby™
- Service
- Results
- Adroit

Schechter Wealth Strategies
- Clients' needs first—always
- A complete "WOW" experience
- A special place to be
- Cutting-edge knowledge—we are the experts

Zoup! Fresh Soup Company
- Action-oriented
- "Can Do" attitude
- No jerks
- Open and honest
- Passion for the brand

Gumby Trademark and Copyright Notice™, and © Premavision, Inc. and Prema Toy Co.

Randall Industries
- Collaboration
- Enthusiastic, energetic, tenacious, and hardworking
- Honesty and integrity
- Humility
- Pride in work
- Ability to adapt/adjust

Professional Grounds Services
- We do whatever it takes in every situation
- We have fun
- We are passionate about our work
- We have integrity in all that we do

Don't run out and tell everyone immediately after you've established your core values. Instead, let them simmer for 30 days and then meet one last time as a team to sign off once and for all on the final list.

The next step in the process is to communicate these core values to the rest of the organization. It's time to create your presentation speech. People won't necessarily understand what you mean if you merely state each core value. That's why each one needs to be backed up with stories, analogies, and creative illustrations to drive home its importance.

When writing your core values speech, make sure you word each core value with the same pattern or tense (e.g., "To always ..." or "We always ..."). Make sure to bullet-point three to five supporting examples under each. This will give you a rough guide of how the speech should be laid out. From there, you can improvise.

Below is an example of an actual outline for a core values speech.

Team-oriented approach
- You can get what you want by helping others get what they want. It's all about service. How can we serve our customers and fellow employees?

- Strive to always act for the greater good of the organization, not our self-interest.

- We should view ourselves as playmakers—a good assist is often more satisfying than getting the goal in sports and at work.

- In sports, team play overcomes raw talent if that talent is not playing together. This applies equally in the work environment.

- We are a team and presently a very good one. Let's together aspire and work to become great!

Commitment to excellence
- As the saying goes, "We only get one chance to make a first impression." Let's make it a good one.

- The written word. It should be clear, concise, and directly to the point. My dad is fond of saying, "If I had more time, I would have written a shorter letter." His point is this: Let every word tell.

- Use we vs. I. Using "we" signifies you are a representative of an organization larger than yourself. The use of "I" can connote ego.

- Be professional when the situation calls for it, and, likewise, feel free to be casual in the right circumstances. Use your emotional intelligence here. However, when in doubt, err on the side of professionalism and conservatism.

- Reputation outweighs profit every time.

Problem-solving approach
- What do we do well? Solve problems.
- How do we solve problems well?
  - Get the facts
  - State the issues correctly and succinctly
  - Ask the right questions
  - Engage in unrestricted but efficient debate

- Listen carefully to all arguments
- Based on relevant facts and persuasive argument decide next course of action
- Assign responsibility for "next steps"
- Promptly execute on agreed-upon course of action
- Follow up on progress at next meeting

- Sometimes a decision is made by not making a decision.

- Sometimes a "wrong decision" produces a better outcome than no decision at all. Velocity of decision-making is often as important as the quality of the decision. Other times protracted contemplation is warranted in order to get the right outcome. This is an art, not a science. Experience counts here.

Candor

- Open and honest communication should be our goal.

- We can all pursue improvement if we are constructively apprised of our strengths and shortcomings.

- Be clear and honest, yet sensitive and supportive.

- Avoid "talking down" to others.

- Seek to communicate with proper balance of confidence and humility.

- When a decision is made that is not in line with your recommendation, simply move on. Don't take it personally. It does not reflect negatively on the value of your input.

Fairness

- Demand results.

- Have a sense of equity. What is a just result under the facts?

- It's OK to be tough when circumstances call for it, but do not take unfair advantage of your strength.

- Be compassionate.

- If you're dealing with a ruthless or unethical opponent, fight hard but always within the rules of engagement. Don't fall into the trap of stooping to his or her level.

Balance

- Work smart. Do what is necessary to get the job done right.

- Valuable output is the greatest measure, not hours put in. Anyone can keep busy, but that does not equate to productivity.

- The story of the accountant who works until 11 p.m. during tax season but has ample time for golf/family in the off-season months—an example of life in balance?

- Volunteer in the community. Always seek to give back. Involve your family.

For more inspiration, here is a complete core value speech as it was delivered to the 51 employees at Wolff Group by the co-owner, Stuart Wolff:

We at Wolff Group are about to embark on our 10-year anniversary! One decade in business as Wolff Group!

But actually, nothing is more important than the number 51.

Yes, 51. That's the number of individuals, people—yes, you— that make up the Wolff Group team, the Wolff Group family. Here are a few more numbers: We could not have been in business for 10 years with four offices in three states as one team if it were not for each and every one of you. Each and every one of you adds something to define who we as Wolff Group are. We are one of the leaders in our industry, yes, but we are so much more.

Enough about numbers, let's use some words. Words such as:

Integrity and honesty

Hard work

Service-oriented

Dedicated

Teamwork

The words above describe us as Wolff Group. These words describe what makes us tick, what drives our passion, what is at our core, the heart of Wolff Group, the heart of us. These words describe a part of each and every one of you.

Why do customers do business with Wolff Group—with a Scott*, with a Tina, with a Bill, with a Lynn, with a Josh, with a Debbie, with a Hank, with a Barb, with a Sean, with a Steve, with a Kelly, just to name a few?

Because these people I just mentioned and all of you understand the importance of treating others with respect, and being honest, sincere, and trustworthy. We know how important ...

Integrity and honesty are to a relationship, any relationship, whether it be a business or personal one. Tie that in with a sincere interest in understanding the needs of our customers, listening to their needs, and being ready to assist when needed. To jump in and help out makes us ...

Service-oriented. This is why when a customer like [ABC Company] calls and tells Tina that the new product is on their menu next week and the supplier is out of stock, Barb stops what she is doing and adds onto the supplier's order to take care of the increased demand for this product. And then again when we find out that the supplier's order is on hold due to a credit issue and Debbie has to stop what she is doing to help get that deduction cleared so the order will ship on time. That shows that we are ...

Dedicated and don't mind **Hard Work**. Then Sean gets an urgent call from [XYZ Company] on a Thursday afternoon saying, "We need you in a sales meeting first thing tomorrow morning with [PDQ Company]." So Sean calls Debbie in a panic to help him out and put together a custom flyer for the next morning that she completes and e-mails to Sean at 1:00 a.m. that night. That proves we thrive on ...

*Names have been changed to protect employee confidentiality.

Teamwork. We respond with a yes, we can do it for you, we can make it happen. This is a team of service-oriented individuals that are focused on their customer needs, work hard, and are ready to do whatever it takes! I can go on sharing more and more stories, but luckily for all of you, I will just name a few.

One thing you will notice about these words is that they're virtues that we can't teach in a class or train you on; they are part of what makes up each and every one of you. It's your core, these are your core values, and it's what makes your heart go pitter-patter every day. Whether it is in your upbringing or in your genes, I am not really sure, but one thing is for sure: People with these virtues are the ones we want to be a part of our team, of our family. Continuing to be committed to finding the right people will be one of the keys to taking Wolff Group to the next level.

Identifying what makes us tick is important, because it lays the groundwork for who we are, where we are going, how we are going to get there, and when. We are on a path that will take us to places we have never been before, and things we have not achieved before. We are on a path that will send us and drive us to wherever we want to go. It is a very exciting time at Wolff Group. I am so glad that each and every one of you is a part of it.

I am driven and dedicated to making the next 10 years at Wolff Group the best ever. I hope you will all join me for this ride—it's going to be fun! Here's to our next decade of blazing a new trail!"

This core value speech was a tipping point for Stu Wolff to catapult his company to four times its size. He delivered this speech five years ago, and since then, with clarity of his culture, he and his partner decided to part ways due to a lack of core value fit. He found a new partner with matching core values.

Once he built a strong culture and crystallized his business model, he then acquired three companies that doubled the size of his company and recently completed the acquisition of an equal-sized company.

Wolff Group is now a $16-million company with a strong culture—very well run and well respected in its industry.

Your core values should become a guiding force in your organization and should be incorporated into your hiring process. When you interview employee candidates, they need to hear that speech. They need to know who you are. It's easy to find people with the right skill set, but you want the one that rows in your direction. You will find that your hiring success ratio will increase if you evaluate applicants' core values before their skill. Every one of my clients follows this exact same process. The reason? It works.

Once your speech is written, delivered, and incorporated into your hiring process, it will become common language within your organization, and that's where your core values will start to come to life. There are many creative ways to keep them alive. For example, one particular client with an amazing culture names each of its conference rooms after a core value. McKinley has a core value called "Gumby." It gave each of its employees a Gumby doll with an attached label explaining that Gumby is flexible, helpful, optimistic, honest and pure, adventurous, fearless, loving, and everybody's friend.

> I've worked with many clients that have acquired other companies, merged with other companies, and have been acquired (incidentally, five of my clients have been acquired, and in every case, they sold for unusually high multiples and the acquiring company said they were the best-run small company they'd ever seen). The number one reason those deals were successful and continue their success is due to core value alignment. I advised every client to start each due-diligence process with core value fit; if there's a fit, everything flows. If not, I advise them not to move forward.

In short, it doesn't matter *what* your core values are as much as it does that you've clearly defined, communicated, and are living them as an organization. Only then can you truly surround yourself with the people who will prepare your organization for growth.

Work on establishing your core values now. Once you're finished, plug them into the V/TO.

CORE VALUES	1. FLEXIBLE 2. INNOVATIVE 3. RESPECTFUL 4. SPIRITED 5. TEAM
CORE FOCUS™	**Purpose/Cause/Passion:** **Our Niche:**

WHAT IS YOUR CORE FOCUS?

It doesn't take much for an organization to get off track in the hustle and bustle of the business world. Businesses can easily become distracted by opportunities that are wolves in sheep's clothing. Others falsely assume that since they are succeeding in one business, they can succeed in any. Others simply get bored.

Your job as a leadership team is to establish your organization's core focus and not to let anything distract you from that. Many things have the potential to distract us from our core focus. Steve, a member of one leadership team, calls it "shiny stuff." A competitor, a new idea, a new product, and poor advice that looks like good advice at the time are just a few examples.

The central concept of a core focus has been given many different names over time, including "mission statement," "vision statement," "core business," "sweet spot," "the zone," and "the ball" (as in "keep your eye on the"). In his book *The 8th Habit*, Stephen Covey calls it "voice." Dan Sullivan calls it Unique Ability®. And in *Good to Great*, Jim Collins calls it "the hedgehog concept." I call it core focus because it should come from your company's core and you must stay laser-focused on it.

Russell H. Conwell's story "Acres of Diamonds" illustrates this point well. To paraphrase: There was once a man named Ali who owned a large farm with many orchards. Ali was perfectly content with his lot in life until one day, when a local priest told him how the Almighty had created diamonds, and how one stone the size of his thumb was worth enough to purchase an entire county. As the story goes, Ali went to bed a poor man. He sold his farm and set out to seek a fortune in diamonds.

After years of searching all over Palestine and Europe and not finding a single diamond, he ended up penniless. In a fit of despair, he threw himself into the raging tide and drowned. Soon afterward, the purchaser of Ali's farm was visited by the same priest that told Ali about diamonds. The priest noticed a small diamond on the mantelpiece and asked, "Where did you find this?" To which the man replied, "There's a brook that runs through our farm, and it's full of them."

Most people are sitting on their own diamond mines. The surest ways to lose your diamond mine are to get bored, become overambitious, or start thinking that the grass is greener on the other side. Find your core focus, stick to it, and devote your time and resources to excelling at it.

When business owners get bored, there is always the potential for them to get distracted by the shiny stuff and inadvertently sabotage what they've created. Fading passion and losing sight of why you're in business are other pitfalls that could lead to the same fate. Defining your core focus will return you to your original levels of clarity and excitement.

A great example of a company distracted by shiny things was Broder & Sachse Real Estate Services Inc. Just prior to starting its EOS process, the real estate management company had dodged a bullet.

This particular bullet came in the form of a business proposal from a man who wanted Broder & Sachse to buy an industrial building he owned so he could start an engine powder-coating company. The deal was that he would lease the building from Broder & Sachse and would use the proceeds of the sale to build the line and the facilities. The man had customers already lined up; he just needed to build the company and open its doors. On paper, it was a million-dollar idea. Excited by the prospect, co-owners Rich Broder and Todd Sachse decided to go one further and partner with the man in the powder-coating business.

After investing a million dollars of their own money and a year and a half of their time, Rich and Todd eventually closed the business. In the three months it had been open, it had lost a total of $300,000. Clearly, it was the worst business decision of their careers. There was, however, a silver lining. Six months later, someone stepped in and bought the company for almost as much as they had put into it. They got lucky. On the other hand, they still lost a year and a half of time and focus on their core business, and that loss is incalculable.

Their mistake is now known around the office as a CCT, which stands for the short-lived company's name: Capital Coating Technologies, Inc. Now, whenever they see something shiny, they jokingly dub it a CCT and direct their energies elsewhere.

Broder & Sachse's core focus is owning and managing real estate, not powder coating. While a new idea may look like a no-brainer on paper, it's simply not worth doing if it's not a part of your core focus.

When your core focus is clear, you're going to come to several important realizations. You'll realize that certain practices, people, and, sometimes, entire divisions and/or product lines don't fit into your core focus. As a direct result of this discovery, past EOS clients have gotten rid of entire departments and excelled as a result.

Once Image One, a $7 million laser printer service and supply company, was clear on its core focus, it eliminated its computer networking business unit and focused entirely on simplifying its clients' printing environments. The decision was a painful and emotional one, but the company did it. As a result, it's grown by an average of 30 percent for every year of the past four, resulting in a sale to a publicly traded company in its industry for high multiples.

Image One's president and co-owner, Rob Dube, says, "The decision to close our computer division after six months was a turning point in our company's history. Once our core focus was clear, there was no turning back." Incidentally Rob and Joel have purchased the business back and continue to grow it at 30 percent per year. Image One was recently selected as the Small Business of the

Year by *Crain's Detroit Business* and also as a finalist for the Ernst & Young Entrepreneur of the Year award.

Decide what business you are in, and be in that business. As the old saying goes, "He who chases two rabbits catches neither." Or as Al Ries pointed out in *Focus*, "Imagine a medical practice saying to itself: 'We are known as terrific brain surgeons, so let's get into the heart, liver, lung, and limb businesses.'"

I'm always amused when a client looks at another industry and says, "I wish I were in that business. It's so much simpler." I'll think to myself, "Oh, if he only knew." In other words, I've yet to see a single business that is easy to run. They *all* take work. Success in one kind of industry doesn't necessarily dictate success in another. You can only succeed in the kind of business that is right for you and your team. As Jim Collins puts it in his bestseller *Good to Great*, "You have to figure out what you're genetically encoded to do." That's a vital point. The combination of your talents and passions combined with your leadership creates something unique that no other company has, and that something is your core focus. You must uncover what it is. The following exercise was designed to help you do just that.

HOW TO DETERMINE YOUR CORE FOCUS

First, you and your leadership team should define, with absolute clarity, your two truths: your reason for being and your niche.

Core focus is actually very simple. Don't overthink it. After reading this section of this book, lock your leadership team in a room for a minimum of two uninterrupted hours. Start by asking them to write the answers to the two questions below. Once everyone has finished, go around the table and have them share what they've written. Then, open up the discussion for debate and talk as a group for as long as you need to.

Do this with both questions, one at a time, until you're on the same page and have each answer down to just a few words. Be warned: You may need several sessions to complete the task. Be patient and remember not to overthink and overanalyze. Like core values, your core focus already exists; it's just a matter of chiseling away the non-core items before you can get it. What follows are the two questions with some real-life examples and tools for guidance:

1. Why does your organization exist?
What is its purpose, cause, or passion?

When your purpose, cause, or passion is clear, you won't be able to tell what business you're in. You should be able to take it into any industry. This will also keep you from confusing it with your niche.

> When entering your core focus into the electronic version of the V/TO, please choose one of the three words "purpose," "passion," or "cause"—the one that resonates best with your team—and delete the others from the document. Less is more.

When your purpose, cause, or passion is clear, it should meet all eight points of the following checklist:

1. It's stated in three to seven words.   ☐

2. It's written in simple language.   ☐

3. It's big and bold.   ☐

4. It has an "aha" effect.   ☐

5. It comes from the heart.   ☐

6. It involves everyone.   ☐

7. It's not about money.   ☐

8. It's bigger than a goal.   ☐

Examples of purposes, causes, or passions
Cunningham/Limp: Customer delight
McKinley: To enrich the quality of life in our communities
Image One: To build a great company, with great people & great results
Schechter Wealth Strategies: To create lifelong relationships and raving fans

2. What is your organization's niche?

Your niche should be simple. It will ultimately become a filtering mechanism for your team to make its decisions as you move forward. Orville Redenbacher's theory says it all: "Do one thing and do it better than anyone."

Examples of niches
Autumn Associates: Creating the right program with right coverage for the right clients
Orville Redenbacher: Popcorn
Atlas Oil Company: Moving gallons
Image One: Simplifying companies' printing environments
McKinley: Solving complex real estate problems

With your niche and your organization's reason for being crystal clear, you now have a core focus. Once your core focus is clear, you'll need to stay true to it. If a new business opportunity doesn't fit, don't do it. If someone on the leadership team tries to throw something incongruent over the wall, throw it back. Let it be your filtering mechanism for all future decisions.

Below are some real-world examples of a company's core focus:

Asphalt Specialists, Inc. (ASI)
Passion: Winning
Niche: Quality asphalt paving

ZenaComp
Passion: Creating efficient solutions
Niche: Worry-free technology that protects & grows our clients' business

Ronnisch Construction Group
Purpose: Exceeding peoples' expectations
Niche: Meeting the schedule in all facets of construction

Image One
Passion: Building a great company, with great people and great results
Niche: Simplifying companies' printing environments

Alongside two other partners, brothers Tyler and Jonathan B. Smith founded a small technology business designing high-end websites with back-end web applications. Once they realized their current business no longer fit their personal core focus, they left the business to their partners and each went on to build successful businesses in line with their core focus.

Jonathan went on to cofound Wave Dispersion Technologies, Inc., a company that provides coastline security for countries all over the world. His company made *Inc.* magazine's list of the 500 fastest-growing private companies.

With his new partner, Brad, Tyler built the web retail company Niche Retail, taking it from start-up to almost $19 million in revenue, in nine years. Tyler and Brad were finalists for the Ernst & Young Entrepreneur of the Year award, and Niche Retail was named #300 on *Inc.* magazine's list of the 500 fastest-growing private companies. Illuminate your core focus, and you could generate those kinds of results as well.

One important point: The task of clarifying your core focus assumes that you already have a financial model that works. If that's the case, it's just a matter of focusing on and executing your vision so that the profit will follow.

If you're a golfer, you know that the face of a golf club has a sweet spot. While its actual size varies depending on the club, let's assume it's about 50 percent of the face. To the degree you hit the ball on the sweet spot, the ball goes farther and straighter, contact feels better, and you'll score better. The same applies to your business. Just like a golf club, your business has a sweet spot, and now that you have clarified your core focus, you now know what it is. Assuming you stay in your sweet spot, which might be about 50 percent of your market, your business will go further and score better in terms of profitability.

Once your core focus is clear, your people, processes, and systems can be put in place to drive it with consistency. Until you have exhausted every opportunity in your core focus, don't allow yourself to get distracted by the shiny stuff.

Now that the work is done, add your core focus to the V/TO.

WHAT IS YOUR 10-YEAR TARGET?

Now that your core values and core focus are clear, the next question is this: What is your 10-year target? Where do you want your organization to be a decade from now?

One common thread unites successful people and successful companies. All of them have a habit of setting and achieving goals. That's why I am consistently amazed by the number of entrepreneurs who can't tell me what their number one goal is. To me, they're like rudderless ships. How do you know if you're heading in the right direction if you don't know which direction you're meant to be going? As Yogi Berra said, "You've got to be careful if you don't know where you are going, 'cause you might not get there."

In their book *Built to Last*, Jim Collins and Jerry I. Porras found that organizations that have endured for decades share another common practice: They all set massive 10- to 25-year goals. Collins and Porras refer to these as BHAGs—Big, Hairy, Audacious Goals—and define them as having "a long-term vision so daring in its scope as to seem impossible."

That's one of the main differences between a 10-year target and any shorter ones you might set. This is the one larger-than-life goal that everyone is working toward, the thing that gives everyone in the organization a long-range direction. Once your 10-year target is clear, you and your leadership team will start doing things differently in the here and now so as to get you there.

In *You*[2], Price Pritchett explains how to make such quantum leaps: "You must focus on ends, rather than means." Your long-term target is that end he is describing. He continues, "It is crucial to have a crystal clear picture of what you want to accomplish ... Rivet your attention on that spot where you are to land at the end of your quantum leap ... Once you do that, it's almost as if you magnetize yourself to the ways and means involved in the methodology for getting there. Solutions begin to appear. Answers come to you."

The reason this particular target's time frame is 10 years is that 90 percent of EOS clients have selected it in the past. Some preferred a five-year time frame, while others went as high as 20 years. The length is entirely up to you.

Examples of 10-year targets
ZenaComp: $10 million in revenue with 15 percent net income
Autumn Associates: A referral from every client and every client from a referral

McKinley: 20,000 multifamily units owned and/or managed
Atlas Oil Company: 5 billion gallons moved
Schechter Wealth Strategies: 15 percent of target market

HOW TO SET A 10-YEAR TARGET

Meet with your leadership team and discuss where you want to take your organization. A word of caution is in order here: While your core values and core focus are already present within your organization, the 10-year target will be different. I've never seen a team land on the same page with a 10-year target on the first go-around. Be patient in your first attempt.

I recommend starting off by asking everyone how far out they would like to look. I would then ask everyone what they believe the revenue size of the organization could be at that point. This is a particularly fun question, and you'll probably get a wide range of responses. These different figures should start to get everyone talking and ultimately in sync with each other. Once those two questions have primed the pump, ask everyone what they believe the target is. It may take a few meetings to settle on a final answer. I've had to come back to certain EOS clients with the same question every quarter until they nailed it.

Once that decision is made, confirm that everyone is motivated by it and on the same page. As with all goal-setting activities, your 10-year target must be specific and measurable so that there can't be any gray areas. You will know the right goal when you have it. It will be the one that creates passion, excitement, and energy for every single person in the organization whenever it's repeated.

> With many clients now closing in on or achieving their 10-year targets, the question regarding what to do when you're getting close to hitting it comes up often. The answer and rule of thumb is that once you're three years from achieving your 10-year target, you move it to your three-year picture (which will be covered on page 66) and set a brand-new one.

Add your 10-year target to the third section of the V/TO.

WHAT IS YOUR MARKETING STRATEGY?

A mother, her young son, and their donkey are taking a long journey through the countryside. The mother is riding the donkey with the son walking alongside as they enter a village. All of a sudden, the village people gather and start stoning them. The pair run away and manage to escape. The mother is dumbfounded, and as they approach the next village, she thinks, "Maybe they thought it was inappropriate to have the son walk," so they switch places and prepare to enter. But once again, they're stoned by the village people. At a total loss, she thinks, "Maybe it's the donkey. Maybe they worship donkeys in this country." So before entering the next village, they decide to pick up the donkey and carry it, but it proves so heavy that as they cross a bridge, the donkey falls over the side, lands in the river, and drowns.

What's the moral of the story? If you try to please everyone, you're going to lose your ass.

I can't tell you how many of my clients start out trying to be all things to all people. They say, "Oh, you need that? Yes, we do that," and, "You want those? No problem." Over time, though, they, their customers, and their employees become frustrated, and the business becomes less profitable. This helter-skelter method may have gotten you to where you are today and helped you survive the early drought, but to break through the ceiling, you have to create some focus.

The intent of this section is to create a laser-sharp focus for your sales and marketing efforts. Many companies waste thousands of dollars on consultancy fees, inconsistent marketing messages, printing, and time, all because they failed to establish a clear strategy from the outset. A focused effort will enable you to sell and close more of the right business. It will become the foundation upon which you create all future materials, plans, messages, and advertising.

This enables you to be different and stand out to your ideal customer. All of your people will have clear direction on who your ideal customer is, what you're supposed to be doing for them, and how you will do it. Ultimately, you will know which customers you should and should not be doing business with. That means you can stop trying to be all things to all people.

In his book *Get Back in the Box: Innovation from the Inside Out*, Douglas Rushkoff makes the point that companies have to stop looking everywhere else for the answers. Rather than hiring marketers and consultants, he urges companies to draw on their own experience, core values, and core competencies (core focus). He urges readers to "stop solving your problems from the outside in." He goes on to say, "Get back in the box and do the thing you actually do best. This disciplined commitment to your own core passion—and not a consultant, ad campaign, or business plan—is the source of true innovation."

Marketing strategy is made up of four elements, which are contained in the fourth section of the V/TO:

1. Your Target Market/"The List"
2. Your Three Uniques
3. Your Proven Process
4. Your Guarantee

YOUR TARGET MARKET
The first element of marketing strategy is your target market, or "The List."

Identifying your target market involves defining your ideal customers. Who are they? Where are they? What are they? You need to know their demographic, geographic, and psychographic characteristics. By identifying your target market, you create a filter. Out of that comes The List of perfect prospects for your organization and sales team to target.

If you're a normal small business, you've probably gotten to where you are with a less-than-perfect approach to finding customers. When you were getting the business off the ground, any customer that paid was considered a good one. As a result, you probably have some customers that are not in your target market. Maybe they're not profitable or they make ridiculous demands. Maybe you don't even like them.

A problem for most companies is that they take a buckshot approach to sales and marketing. By defining your target market and creating The List, you're abandoning the shotgun approach for the rifle approach. As a result, your sales and marketing efforts will be much more efficient.

A crucial step to getting sales back on track during the turnaround of our real estate sales training company involved determining who our ideal target market was. Eventually, we realized that it was the presidents and CEOs of real estate organizations with 200 or more agents (demographic) in North America (geographic) that saw the value and need for outside sales training (psychographic).

With this clarity, we ran the filter (which meant that we researched every industry publication, database, and resource) to find out who and how many there were. We came up with a total of 525. At our next quarterly meeting with all of our trainers, we did a skit with a biblical theme that included music and dress. We created a large binder with The List on the cover. It contained contact information and relevant details on 525 presidents and CEOs.

We distributed those names to our 30 trainers, who were our sales force, and they went to work. By focusing on The List, we were able to turn sales around. Ultimately, we were able to penetrate and maintain over 50 percent of The List as our clients. This was not an anomaly. Every client that defines its target market creates this laser focus as a result.

Examples

Image One: IT directors in companies with 25 or more laser printers in Michigan and Ohio

McKinley: Opportunistic, value-added, or underperforming apartments, shopping centers, and office buildings in Michigan, Indiana, Ohio, Illinois, Virginia, Georgia, and Florida

Identity Marketing and Public Relations: Small to mid-sized privately held business-to-business companies in the U.S. that meet our profile

Defining your target market is rewarding. The difference in my clients' attitude and awareness after doing so is like night and day. Where they used to try to lasso every customer in sight, they now know in the first 15 minutes of talking to a prospect whether they are right or not. As a result, they are bringing on better clients with less hassles and more profit. They no longer waste valuable time with prospects that are not right for them. In addition, they've dropped existing customers that are not in their target market and creating stress via unreasonable demands and low profitability.

How to Make The List

Have everyone on the leadership team brainstorm what they believe to be the following:

- The geographic characteristics of your ideal customers. Where are they?

- The demographic characteristics of your ideal customers. What are they? (If you're marketing business-to-business, consider characteristics such as job title, industry, size, and type of business. If business-to-consumer, then age, sex, income or profession.)

- The psychographic characteristics of your ideal customers. How do they think? What do they need? What do they appreciate?

With the answers to these questions, go to work on creating The List, which consists of the key contact information for each prospect. I won't kid you— creating The List will take some work. It involves a combination of examining your current prospect lists, generating referrals from existing clients, reading trade publications, purchasing lists, asking around, and telling your salespeople to keep their ears to the ground. You have to harvest and then stockpile these names in a database. Once they're compiled, your sales/marketing manager has a list of all of your prospects in one place or at least knows where they are and manages them accordingly, confirming that the sales and marketing efforts are laser-focused on them.

Determine the best way to reach these people by using your newly clarified marketing strategy, which you will complete at the end of this section. Most companies realize that the best way to reach their newly clarified target market is through referrals, using their clients to connect with their prospects. You have a variety of options to reach your target market; it all depends on the best approach for your company. McKinley uses banking relationships; Image One uses a combination of cold calls, referrals, and direct mail; and ZenaComp uses networking. Once you're clear on your core values, core focus, 10-year target, and marketing strategy, the answer should present itself. With this clarity, you can move forward with a targeted approach to your sales and marketing efforts. That will create a growing snowball until you reach a point at which the sales effort becomes self-perpetuating. The task of generating new business will then require considerably less effort than it did in the beginning.

Add your Target Market to the V/TO.

YOUR THREE UNIQUES

Other common marketing terms for this are "differentiators" and "value proposition." Plainly put, these are what make you different, what make you stand out, and what you're competing with. If you line yourself up against 10 of your competitors, you might all share one of these uniques. Some of you may even share two, but no one else should have the three you do. You need to settle on three qualities that will truly make your company unique to the ideal customer.

Again, what you're creating here is focus. The most common mistake that most organizations make involves competing in too many sectors, markets, services, or product lines, and trying to be all things to all people. It's a game you will not win.

Rather than your salespeople saying, "Yes, we do that, and oh yes, we'll do that," to everything, they should be saying, "If you're looking for that, we probably aren't the company for you. What we excel at are these three things." The reality is that if those people don't want what you have to offer, they're not the right clients for you in the first place. In the end, you're both going to end up unhappy anyway.

Southwest Airlines is a great example of this. It focuses on low fares, on-time flights, and having fun. That's what drives everything in that organization's business model. If you've flown on Southwest, you know it doesn't offer any frills. As a result, it doesn't appeal to everyone, but that's okay. Southwest matters to its ideal customer and that's all that counts.

In the company's book *Nuts! Southwest Airlines' Crazy Recipe for Business and Personal Success* is a story about a woman who sent Southwest a complaint letter after every flight she took. She would complain about problems such as the lack of assigned seating, the lack of a first-class section, the lack of meals, the flight attendants' uniforms, and the casual atmosphere. According to the book, one of the letters made it up to the desk of then-CEO Herb Kelleher. It took him 60 seconds to write back the following note: "Dear Mrs. Crabapple, we will miss you. Love, Herb."

If you believe in your Three Uniques, and you believe they matter to your ideal customer, you should never apologize for them.

How to Choose Your Three Uniques

For this step, you might consider including your sales team in the marketing strategy sessions. List everything that you believe makes your people, company, product, or service. What do your ideal customers think is unique about you? Ask them—it's a 10-minute phone call.

Through the process of elimination, make some tough decisions. Debate and decide which are the three that truly make you unique, and which matter to you and your customer. The individual uniques don't have to be different from those of your competition. It's the combination of all Three Uniques that makes you different. No one else should do all three the way you do.

Examples

Identity Marketing and Public Relations (a PR and marketing firm)
1. We get what you do
2. We generate results
3. Full-house, in-house

McKinley (property management)
1. High touch customer service and sales
2. We invest in our people
3. We take an owner's perspective

Autumn Associates (property and casualty insurance)
1. Our people/core values
2. By referral only
3. Client-selection process

Add your Three Uniques to the V/TO.

YOUR PROVEN PROCESS

My dad always teaches, "Never tell someone something you can show them." In most companies, when salespeople are meeting with a prospective new customer, they normally try to win new business by using countless words and visuals in the form of pages and charts. When it's all said and done, they end up looking just like everyone else.

There is a proven way you provide your service or product to your customers. You do it every time, and it produces the same result. It's what got you where you are. What you need to do is capture that process in a visual format to guide your sales team. It should be encompassed on one single piece of paper, it must illustrate your proven process, and it must have a name. It should show each step, from the first client interaction to the ongoing follow-up once your product or service has been delivered.

There are typically three to seven major steps in any company's proven process. The EOS Process is shown on the next page as an example. Creating a standard proven process to use in selling situations will give you two very powerful advantages. It will increase your potential customers' confidence and peace of mind in doing business with you. Second, as most other companies don't illustrate how they work, it will makes you stand out among the competition.

Rather than giving them a sales presentation and inundating them with information, you're saying, "Let me show you exactly how we are able to accomplish great results for our customers. We have a proven process that we follow called The (your company name) Difference."

An ancillary benefit of creating your proven process is that it will help your organization internally. Each person in the organization will know how his or her actions affect the customer and why his or her step in the process is important.

How to Create Your Proven Process
Step 1

With your team, illustrate on a whiteboard what you believe are the major steps in your proven process and then give each step a name. These major steps are the touch points with your customers when you interface with them. The rule of thumb is three to seven steps.

Example

It took financial services company Schechter Wealth Strategies about three hours to create its proven process. After much discussion and debate, the team agreed they had six steps in their proven process:

1. Discovery
2. Solution Presentation I
3. Competitive Bidding
4. Solution Presentation II
5. Solution Implementation
6. Review and Service

Step 2

Once your steps have been determined, add two to five bullets under each item for your salespeople to use as talking points when selling to a prospective customer. For example, in Schechter's case, under Step 1, there are three bullets: (1) about us, (2) about you, and (3) defining your objectives.

Step 3

Give your proven process a name. If you cannot come up with a name, simply call it "Our Proven Process" or "The (your company name) Difference," as many EOS clients do.

Step 4

Once you've hammered out your proven process, turn your work over to a graphic designer to give it a visual based on your company's colors, logo, and look and feel. As a result of all the work you've done, this should be relatively inexpensive. The graphic designer simply needs to design your proven process in a way that is appealing to you, your people, and your customers.

Step 5

Have it professionally printed, in color, on a heavy stock, and/or laminated. This will increase the perceived value considerably in the eyes of your prospective customers.

Add the name of your Proven Process to the V/TO.

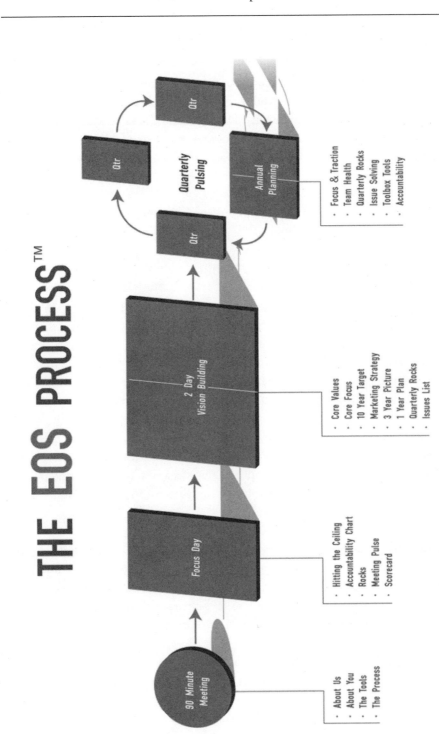

THE EOS PROCESS™

90 Minute Meeting
- About Us
- About You
- The Tools
- The Process

Focus Day
- Hitting the Ceiling
- Accountability Chart
- Rocks
- Meeting Pulse
- Scorecard

2 Day Vision Building
- Core Values
- Core Focus
- 10 Year Target
- Marketing Strategy
- 3 Year Picture
- 1 Year Plan
- Quarterly Rocks
- Issues List

Quarterly Pulsing

Qtr

Qtr

Qtr

Annual Planning
- Focus & Traction
- Team Health
- Quarterly Rocks
- Issue Solving
- Toolbox Tools
- Accountability

YOUR GUARANTEE

The fourth and final element of your marketing strategy is your guarantee. Think of what Federal Express did with overnight delivery: "When it absolutely, positively has to be there overnight." Domino's did the same with pizza delivery: "Thirty minutes or it's free." Now hospital ERs are adopting the idea with waiting room times, guaranteeing a wait of 30 minutes or less. Some even guarantee no wait at all.

A guarantee is your opportunity to pinpoint an industry-wide problem and solve it. This is typically a service or quality problem. You must determine what your customers can count on from you. If you guarantee it, that will put their minds at ease and enable you to close more business.

Some businesses are not suitable for guarantees. Fifty percent of EOS clients do not have guarantees because they haven't been able to come up with a great one that will drive more business. You will not go out of business without a guarantee, but you will attain your vision faster with one. You're actually closing less business now because you're not entirely putting your prospective customers' minds at ease. If you can do that, you will gain more customers.

Image One came up with a guarantee that it has been capitalizing on for over eight years. The biggest single problem its customers faced in the laser printer service business was losing days of productivity as a result of their printers being down. Co-owner Joel Pearlman solved it by guaranteeing, "Four hours or it's free."

Your guarantee has a secondary benefit. It forces all the people in your organization to deliver on it. That in turn forces you to look inward and make sure you've got all the right people, processes, and systems in place to do so. If not, you'll be forced to improve upon it. Your client will never need to make good on that guarantee if you're at your absolute best.

How to Select Your Guarantee

Brainstorm with your leadership team and list what you believe to be the biggest frustrations, fears, and worries for your potential customer when doing business with you. The ideal guarantee is backed up by a tangible penalty if you don't deliver on it. Your guarantee must drive more business or enable you to close more of what you're not winning. If it doesn't, you shouldn't waste your time using it.

It's a good idea to ask a few ideal current customers or prospects for their feedback. Sometimes my clients have a hard time with the word "guarantee." In these cases, call it a pledge, commitment, or promise. This seems to move the creative thinking process forward.

List all the possible guarantees you'd be willing to offer that will put your potential customers' minds at ease and close more business. From there, choose the best one. If it meets all of the above criteria and you believe it is the right one, then roll it out.

You may not get this one on the first try. Be patient and the right guarantee will come. The awareness alone will start to give you and your team ideas. For example, I was driving by a collision shop the other day and saw that it had a banner that read, "Free Loaners." It's addressing its customers' biggest frustration: being without a car. On the radio, I heard a mortgager guarantee any loan in 14 days or you get $500. Once you're aware of them, you'll see and hear guarantees everywhere. Yours will come.

Add your guarantee to the V/TO.

Now that the four elements of your marketing strategy are clearly defined, it's time to pull the entire marketing strategy section together. You can now clearly communicate a consistent marketing strategy for the entire organization to support, which clarifies for everyone what they must deliver. This becomes the foundation for all of your sales and marketing materials, messages, and presentations moving forward.

Go after all of the prospects on The List, communicating with them why you're unique, showing them your proven process for doing business, and offering them your guarantee. This incredible precision in your sales and marketing efforts will increase your sales dramatically.

WHAT IS YOUR THREE-YEAR PICTURE?

With the first four sections of the V/TO complete, you now know who you are, what you are, where you're going, and what marketing strategy you're going to use to get there. It's now time to illustrate what your business will look like three short years from now.

With life and business moving as fast as it does in the 21st century, there is little value in detailed strategic planning beyond a three-year window. A lot can change during that time span. For the investment of time and money into that kind of planning, there is typically very little return. It's still valuable, however, to create a picture of the future organization three years out. This will accomplish two vital objectives. First, your people will be able to "see" what you're saying and determine if they want to be part of that scenario. Assuming they do, if they can see the vision, it's more likely to happen. Second, it greatly improves the one-year planning process. With the three-year picture clearly in mind, you can more easily determine what you have to do in the next 12 months to stay on track. As Napoleon Hill said, "Whatever the mind of man can conceive and believe, it can surely achieve."

As you can see on the V/TO, the three-year picture is composed of measurables at the top and bullet points to create the picture. It's simple but powerful. Do not underestimate the importance of this section, but also don't overthink it. You're painting a picture of the destination, not discussing every obstacle along the way.

PAINT THE THREE-YEAR PICTURE

Schedule an hour with your leadership team. Once you're assembled, have a copy of the V/TO placed in front of each member. Begin by selecting a future date. I recommend keeping it within the end of the calendar year, thus making it easier for people to envision.

Next, determine the revenue picture. Start by asking your team this question: What is the annual revenue going to be three years from now? This is always fun, because you find out if your leadership is in sync with how fast you want to grow. You will typically get a range, but you'll have to settle at one number. One new client's range was between $20 million and $100 million. Can you imagine how different those individual future views must have been? They can't coexist in the same company without creating complexity, confusion, and frustration. That client eventually got everyone on the same page with a figure of $30 million.

Wolff Group originally had a range of $10 to 25 million, with two co-owners at either end of the spectrum. At the time, it was a $4 million company with 51 employees. Through much discussion, debate, and study, it settled on $15 million, and both owners, along with the entire leadership team, ended up on the same page and equally excited for their future. The need to create a three-year picture becomes more and more evident every time I work with a client.

The next step is to agree on the profit number. This will be a similar conversation, but should be settled much more quickly. After that, you'll want to determine your specific measurables. Measurables give everyone scope and size. Every organization has one or two very specific figures that are a telltale sign of the size of the organization. It might be a number of clients, large clients, units, or widgets produced.

Atlas Oil Company supplies fuel to gas stations, and its measurable is gallons. Last year, it moved 725 million gallons. In its three-year picture, its measurable is over a billion. This number shows scope and size, and it forces the team to think about what it will take to almost double the size of the organization in three years. Equally as important, it confirms that the leadership is in agreement and ready for that type of growth. Another example is Zoup!, a company that franchises a casual soup-and-sandwich concept. Its measurable is its number of stores. Last year, Zoup! had 38 stores; its three-year picture measurable is 94.

Once you've determined your numbers, have everyone on the leadership team take a few minutes and write down bullet points of what the organization will look like on that date three years from now. Factors to consider include things such as number and quality of people, added resources, office environment and size, operational efficiencies, systemization, technology needs, product mix, and client mix.

Combine these results, and after some discussion and debate, your three-year picture will typically contain 10 to 20 bullet points that describe what your organization will look like. In addition, each person on the leadership team should verbalize his or her vision for his or her individual role in the organization in that time frame. You'll gain some interesting insights into people's motivations and help get everyone's expectations in line.

You cannot move on and finalize your three-year picture until everyone on the leadership team sees it clearly. At this point, everyone in the room should close his or her eyes as one person reads the three-year picture out loud. The picture must be visible in each person's mind. Each must believe in it and ultimately want it. After all, they are the team that needs to make it happen. In this session, encourage people to speak up, debate and go back and forth, but ultimately they must agree on all of the major points. You now have a three-year picture that you can take to your organization at large.

Add your three-year picture to the V/TO.

WHAT IS YOUR ONE-YEAR PLAN?
We're now going to the traction side of the V/TO, which is about bringing your long-range vision down to the ground and making it real. That means deciding on what must get done this year.

Remember, less is always more. Most companies make the mistake of trying to accomplish too many objectives per year. By trying to get everything done all at once, they end up accomplishing very little and feeling frustrated. One client of mine was very stubborn about this point for the first two years. I would tell him to limit the company goals between three and seven, and each year we set goals, he would keep piling on more. When we were done, the company would have 12 to 15 goals for the year. Like clockwork, at the end of the year, they would accomplish very little and end up frustrated. Going into the third year, he finally had a revelation: They were taking on too much. With this awareness, we agreed that the team could choose only three goals for the coming year. They did, and by the end of the year, they accomplished all three, increased sales by 19 percent, and had their most profitable year in five years. When everything is important, nothing is important. The EOS approach is going to force you to focus on a few goals rather than too many. By doing that, you will actually accomplish more. That is the power of focus.

HOW TO CREATE YOUR ONE-YEAR PLAN

Schedule two hours with your leadership team. When everyone is sitting at the table, decide on the future date. It's highly recommended you keep within either a calendar year or your fiscal year, regardless of where you are in the year. So, if it's July, set your future date as December 31. After that time, you'll be able to set a brand-new full one-year plan. Having a partial-year plan allows you to gain experience with the process between now and then.

As with the three-year picture, again, decide on the numbers. What is your annual revenue goal? What is your profit goal? What is the measurable? This number should be consistent with the three-year picture measurable.

With the three-year picture in mind, discuss, debate, and decide on the three to seven most important priorities that must be completed this year in order for you to be on track for your three-year picture. These become your goals. They need to be specific, measurable, and attainable. This is an important point. I cannot tell you how many times when reviewing one-year goals at the end of the year, I observe clients debating what the goal actually meant. To avoid this, the goal must be specific, leaving no wiggle room. An outsider should be able to read it and know what it means. Remember, measurable means you can measure it. "Sales" is not a specific goal, but "$1 million in new sales" is. "Improve customer satisfaction" is not a specific goal, but "increase average customer rating to a 9" is.

"Attainable" means that it's doable. Setting unrealistic goals is the biggest trap entrepreneurs fall into. The team has to believe it's possible to hit the goal, or else you can't hold someone accountable to it. If every goal is a "stretch goal," how do you know what success is? Goals are set to be achieved.

Make sure you have a projected budget in place that supports your one-year plan. Many companies set goals for the year with no financial projection to confirm that the plan is even feasible. A budget will force you to confirm that you have all of the resources you need to achieve the plan and that when you achieve the revenue goal, the profit number is realistic. Almost every time a profit goal is first projected, the discussion lowers the number as reality is brought to bear.

Add your one-year plan to the V/TO.

WHAT ARE YOUR QUARTERLY ROCKS?

Once your one-year plan is clear, you need to narrow your vision all the way down to what really matters: the next 90 days. You should determine what the most important priorities are in the coming quarter. Those priorities are called Rocks.

Quarterly Rocks create a 90-Day World for your organization, a powerful concept that enables you to gain tremendous traction. How do they work? Every 90 days, your leadership team comes together to establish its priorities for the next 90 days based on your one-year plan. You discuss and ultimately conclude what has to be executed in the next quarter to put you on track for the one-year plan, which in turn puts you on track for the three-year picture, and so on.

In a growing organization, it's normal to battle for resources, time, and attention. There will be tension. But when you have finished setting your Rocks and all the dust has settled, you should all be united on what objectives take precedence in the coming quarter. The focus of the Rocks is what makes this process so productive. Most organizations enter the next quarter battling on all fronts. They make everything a priority and accomplish very little. By setting Rocks every quarter as a team, you gain considerably more traction and finally reach your goals.

The complete process of setting Rocks is addressed in Chapter 8. Once they are set, add them to your V/TO.

WHAT ARE YOUR ISSUES?

The eighth and final section in the V/TO is the Issues List. While it may seem strange to include a list of problems as part of your vision, that list is actually as important as the previous seven questions. Now that you clearly know where you're going, you have to identify all of the obstacles that could prevent you from reaching your targets.

The sooner you accept that you have issues, the better off you're going to be. You will always have them; your success is in direct proportion to your ability to solve them. Your leadership team should state them openly and honestly so that you can get them out of your heads and into writing. In doing so, you're taking the first step to solving them.

HOW TO IDENTIFY YOUR ISSUES

This exercise can be done very quickly, in 15 minutes at most. Ask the team to think of the obstacles, concerns, and opportunities you face in achieving your vision. From there, let the opinions fly. Don't sugarcoat them. Encourage an open atmosphere where they can all come out.

Through answering the eight questions laid out in this chapter as a team, most of the issues will emerge. They'll come up when your team says something like, "But what about ..." and, "We can't do that because ..." or, "Bill won't buy into it because ..." These are all issues. By the end of this book, you'll have developed a sixth sense for capturing issues. From there, you will develop a discipline for adding them to the Issues List. You'll know when the Issues List truly has become a habit, because the next time you get hit with an obstacle, you'll simply say, "There's another one," and add it to the list.

After all of the issues are out in the open, add them to the V/TO Issues List. Don't worry about solving them yet. That will be addressed in Chapter 6.

You have answered all eight questions, your vision is clear, and your V/TO is complete. An example of what yours might look like follows.

THE VISION/TRACTION ORGANIZER™

ORGANIZATION NAME:

VISION

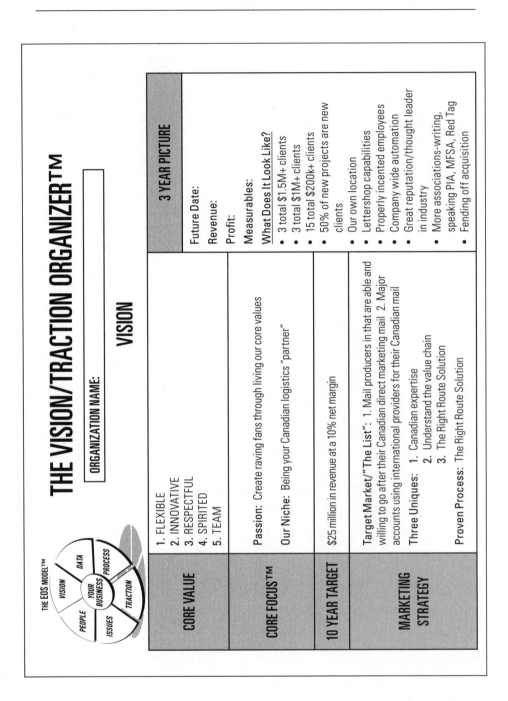

THE EOS MODEL™

CORE VALUE	1. FLEXIBLE 2. INNOVATIVE 3. RESPECTFUL 4. SPIRITED 5. TEAM
CORE FOCUS™	**Passion:** Create raving fans through living our core values **Our Niche:** Being your Canadian logistics "partner"
10 YEAR TARGET	$25 million in revenue at a 10% net margin
MARKETING STRATEGY	**Target Market/"The List":** 1. Mail producers in that are able and willing to go after their Canadian direct marketing mail 2. Major accounts using international providers for their Canadian mail **Three Uniques:** 1. Canadian expertise 2. Understand the value chain 3. The Right Route Solution **Proven Process:** The Right Route Solution

3 YEAR PICTURE

Future Date:

Revenue:

Profit:

Measurables:

What Does It Look Like?
- 3 total $1.5M+ clients
- 3 total $1M+ clients
- 15 total $200k+ clients
- 50% of new projects are new clients
- Our own location
- Lettershop capabilities
- Properly incented employees
- Company wide automation
- Great reputation/thought leader in industry
- More associations–writing, speaking PIA, MFSA, Red Tag
- Fending off acquisition

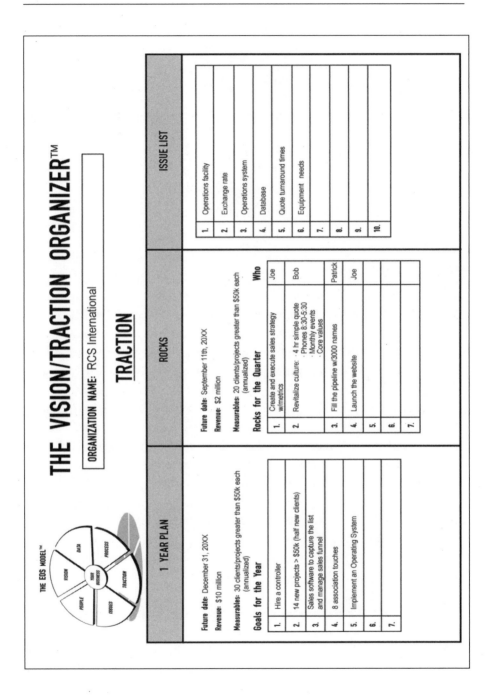

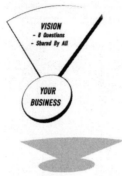

SHARED BY ALL

Now that you have completed your V/TO—the first part of the Vision Component—the foundation for the rest of The EOS Process is set. The second part is to share your vision with your employees. The number one reason employees don't share a company vision is that they don't know what it is. The only way you can determine if your vision is shared by all is simply to tell them.

A Harris Interactive/FranklinCovey poll of over 23,000 employees in key industries and employed in key functional areas sheds a sharp light on this issue. The poll revealed that 37 percent of employees didn't understand their companies' priorities. Only one in five was enthusiastic about their organization's goals, and only one in five saw a clear connection between their tasks and their organization's goals.

Now that your vision is on paper, you must communicate it to everyone in the organization, and every person must understand it and share it. When everyone's energy is going in the same direction, their accumulated drive will kick in and create an exponential force.

Don't be afraid to let your people challenge the vision and ask questions. These inquisitions, along with the preceding dialogue, will help you both become more invested in the vision. While you may worry that they may point out a flaw in the plan, that's not a bad thing at all. If they notice and highlight a potential problem, they'll be even more committed as a result of their involvement in the resulting exchange and resolution. Be willing to be vulnerable.

Here's the brutal truth: Not everyone in your organization will share your vision. The responsibility that you have as the leadership team is to share your V/TO and inspire your people with a compelling vision. As long as they understand it, they want to be a part of it, and their actions perpetuate the vision, they share it. The ones that don't will stand out by contrast. Most of the time, they'll leave before you have to let them go. But as a good manager, you'll be doing them and others in the company a disservice by keeping them around. You may have to help free up the futures of the ones that don't willingly leave.

You can effectively communicate the company vision in three events:

1. Have a company kickoff meeting and unveil your clearly defined vision (the V/TO). This is an opportunity to share your newly created core value speech for the first time. Make sure to include question-and-answer time.

2. Every 90 days, have a short (no more than 45-minute) state-of-the-company meeting with all employees. The objective of this event is to share successes and progress, review the V/TO, and communicate newly set company Rocks for the quarter.

> The quarterly state-of-the-company has proven to be the most effective discipline for helping people share, understand, and buy into the company vision. In its purest form, the meeting has a three-part agenda.
>
> > 1. Where you've been
> > 2. Where you are
> > 3. Where you are going
>
> Each quarter, you and your leadership team fill each of those agenda items with three of the most relevant data points, and you'll deliver a clear, concise, and powerful message that keeps your people in the know. Its effectiveness stems from delivering it every quarter and being consistent.

3. Each quarter, as you set Rocks in each department, conduct a complete review of the V/TO as a team.

Each of these three events will prompt questions and answers that continuously clarify the vision for everyone. You'll need to give people the opportunity to ask questions and understand the vision. As a result, they'll be able to decide if this is the company they want to be a part of. Through that process, they'll be able to direct themselves. The core values, core focus, and marketing strategy will always give them clear direction on their actions and enable them to make better decisions on their own, further enabling you to delegate and elevate.

People need to hear the vision seven times before they really hear it for the first time. Human beings have short attention spans and are a little jaded when it comes to new messages. As a good leader, you must remain consistent in your message. The first time they hear it, they'll roll their eyes and say, "Here we go again." (Remember, you created this culture through past inconsistencies.) The second time, they'll still roll their eyes a little. But by the fourth and fifth time of hearing it, they'll realize this is for real. By the seventh time, they'll be on board. You'll have to adjust your outlook from "I've told them three times—this is so frustrating!" to "I've told them three times—only four more to go!" Be patient, and remember that this is a journey.

Here are some additional real-life examples of how companies share their vision with employees:

RE/MAX First: Each member of the seven-person leadership team took 12 people apiece (84 total), taught them one-on-one, and quizzed them on their Three Uniques.

McKinley: Took their 12 mid-managers, divided them among the leadership team members, and mentored them.

The Professional Group: Conducted on-the-spot core value checks. If someone could name them all, they'd receive a $20 bill on the spot.

Other EOS clients have enlarged the V/TO and posted it somewhere in the office for everyone to see.

I also learned of a company that offered a weekly $20 gift card, albeit with a unique twist. The employee that received it the previous week would give it to the next employee who exhibited one of the company's core values. They had to e-mail the entire organization and tell everyone who they gave it to and what core value that person exhibited. The gift card could never go to the same employee until everyone received it, and it had to cross departments each time. In 52 weeks, that company spread 52 core value stories.

You achieve your full potential when your leadership team is on the same page with answers to the eight questions. Everyone in the organization shares the company vision, wants to be a part of it, and perpetuates it with his or her actions and words.

Now you must start to make the vision a practical reality.

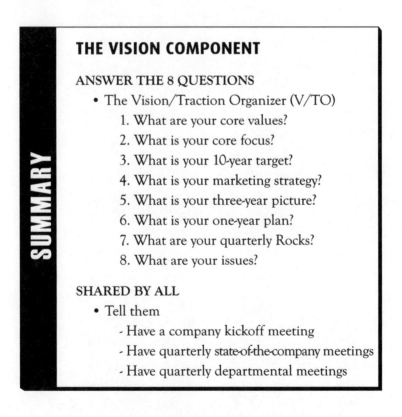

SUMMARY

THE VISION COMPONENT

ANSWER THE 8 QUESTIONS
- The Vision/Traction Organizer (V/TO)
  1. What are your core values?
  2. What is your core focus?
  3. What is your 10-year target?
  4. What is your marketing strategy?
  5. What is your three-year picture?
  6. What is your one-year plan?
  7. What are your quarterly Rocks?
  8. What are your issues?

SHARED BY ALL
- Tell them
  - Have a company kickoff meeting
  - Have quarterly state-of-the-company meetings
  - Have quarterly departmental meetings

CHAPTER 4

THE
PEOPLE COMPONENT

SURROUND YOURSELF
WITH GOOD PEOPLE

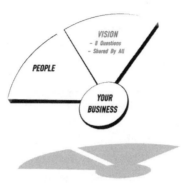

Have you ever noticed that great leaders frequently credit their success to having "good people"? What the heck does that even mean? Whenever I asked these leaders what exactly that meant, I seemed to get a different answer every time. Eventually, I realized that the answers were all exactly the same. Sure, the words were different, but the context never changed. In this chapter, I'll cut through all the confusing terminology such as "good people," "A players," "platinum," "top quartile," and "superstars," and get to the root of the matter.

It all comes down to getting the right people in the right seats. Jim Collins made this idea very popular in his bestseller *Good to Great*. It's an idea that has been around for a long time. Unfortunately, there has never been a crystal clear definition for what it actually means. As a result, it was another term among a complex mix of terminologies that only added to the confusion. And yet the definition is actually quite simple.

The right people are the ones who share your company's core values. They fit and thrive in your culture. They are people you enjoy being around and who make your organization a better place to be. A perfect example is the receptionist for Autumn Associates. As she returned home from vacation, her flight was delayed for so long that her plane landed only an hour before she was due back to work for an 8:00 a.m. meeting. The employees had created a custom of wearing logo apparel to all company meetings, so she had her mother pick her up from the airport with her company shirt. She changed in the car and was at work on time, apparel and all. This exemplified two of the company's core values—commitment and caring. In this chapter you will be introduced to your second EOS tool, the People Analyzer, which will cut through the murkiness of personnel choices to show you who's right for your company.

Core Values + People Analyzer = Right People

The right seat means that each of your employees is operating within his or her area of greatest skill and passion inside your organization and that the roles and responsibilities expected of each employee fit with his or her *Unique Ability*®.[1] This is a concept created by Dan Sullivan and is a registered trademark of The Strategic Coach, Inc. In the book *Unique Ability*, authors Catherine Nomura, Julia Waller, and Shannon Waller explain that everyone has a Unique Ability®. The trick is to discover yours. When you're operating from within your Unique Ability®, your superior skill is often noticed by others who value it. You experience never-ending improvement, feel energized rather than drained, and, most of all, you have a passion for what you're doing that presses you to go further than others would in this area. When this combination of passion and talent finds the right audience, it naturally creates value for others, who, in return, offer you greater rewards and more opportunities for further improvement. It's like your personal core focus. When a person is operating in his or her Unique Ability®, he or she is in the right seat.

One of the obstacles in gaining traction and achieving your vision is that roles, responsibilities, expectations, and job descriptions are unclear due to structural issues. A hazy structure may have gotten you to where you are, but it will not take you any further. A common mistake entails creating a structure to accommodate people you like or don't want to lose. When creating a structure to function efficiently, you must take the long view. Sometimes this means eliminating or changing seats that are no longer relevant. To break through the ceiling, you must make sure you have the right structure in place to get you to the next level. That leads us to the Accountability Chart, the ultimate tool for structuring your organization the right way, defining roles and responsibilities, and clearly identifying all of the seats in the organization.

---

[1]The Strategic Coach and Unique Ability® are trademarks and integral concepts owned by The Strategic Coach, Inc. Unique Ability® and its derivative works are copyrights owned by The Strategic Coach, Inc. All rights reserved. Used with written permission. www.strategiccoach.com.

Unique Ability® + Accountability Chart = Right Seats

As you move forward, you'll be faced with two types of issues regarding your people. The first is having the right person in the wrong seat. The second is having the wrong person in the right seat. In order to gain traction, you'll need to address both. Let's look at them one at a time.

RIGHT PERSON, WRONG SEAT

In this case, you have the right person (i.e., one who shares your core values), but he or she is truly not operating in his or her Unique Ability®. This person has been promoted to a seat that is too big, has outgrown a seat that is too small, or has been put in a position that does not utilize his or her Unique Ability®. Generally, this person is where he or she is because he or she has been around a long time, you like him or her, and he or she is a great addition to the team. Until now, you probably believed you were helping this person by promoting him or her to his or her existing seat. In actuality, you were hindering his or her growth and the growth of the company. Your job in this situation is to move this person out of that seat and into a seat that is right for this person, one where he or she will be successful.

Assuming that there is such a seat—and most of the time, there is—the problem is solved once you move this person. Unfortunately, sometimes there is no seat available. In this case, you have to make a very difficult choice. You have to make decisions for the greater good of the business, and you don't have the luxury of keeping people around simply because you like them. If this is the case, you must let them go. This will be one of the toughest issues you will have to face. Once the change is made, the company is always better off, and usually the person is happier in the long run.

WRONG PERSON, RIGHT SEAT

In this case, the person excels at what he or she does, is extremely productive, and is clearly in his or her Unique Ability®. What makes this person the wrong person is that he or she doesn't share your core values. While this obstacle may seem like something you can live with in the short term, that person is killing your organization in the long run. He or she is chipping away at what you're trying to build, in little ways that, most of the time, you don't even see. It's that wry comment in the hallway, the dirty look behind your back, and the dissension that this person spreads.

Early in the process, one client had a wrong person, right seat issue. The company's top salesperson was a man without integrity. While he was very friendly, professional in his approach, and knowledgeable, he constantly shaded the truth to make sure he had the successful quote. His new business growth was 20 percent per year, and his clients never complained. Because the leadership team had not identified their core values yet, they let the situation drag on for 12 months. As they realized how he was building the business, they faced a seemingly difficult decision. Only after letting him go did their employees and vendors open up about their feelings and concerns. He was damaging the company's reputation the entire time he worked for it. Their core values were now in writing, and they included integrity. "Never again will we allow an employee to work for us without living this core value," the owner stated.

No matter how difficult the issue is, you have to make a good business decision here for the long haul. If you have a wrong person in the right seat, ultimately that person must go for the sake of the greater good.

Of course, there is a third type of people issue, and that is wrong person, wrong seat. The solution is obvious: That person must go. But the way you reached that point isn't always obvious. Another client had a CFO for more than 20 years. In the beginning, he shared the core values, was talented, and was absolutely in the right seat. As time went on, the business, industry, and technology changed, and he didn't change with them. The seat was outgrowing him. His attitude also changed considerably. He became resentful, aloof, and less friendly than he used to be. He was no longer the right person or in the right seat. The owners had not noticed the change until the core values and the right structure were clarified and put in place. They wrestled with the thorny issue for a year and a half, all the while giving their CFO chances to change with the times and adopt the new core values, to no avail. Left with no other choice, they replaced him with a new CFO. The difference was like night and day. Their sessions were considerably more productive, the finance department finally got reorganized, and the company positioned itself to make the next leap ahead.

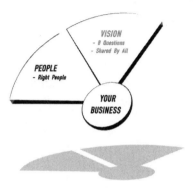

Your job is to hire, fire, review, reward, and recognize all of your people around core values and Unique Abilities®. That's the way to build an organization with all of the right people in the right seats.

Let's see how this can be done in practical terms. The following tools will enable you to assess your people and make the right choices. We'll turn first to Right People and then to Right Seats.

RIGHT PEOPLE

With the answer to the first question on the V/TO—"What are your core values?"—you now have the ability to define who the right people are for your organization. It's important to note that whatever your core values are, they don't make the people who don't possess them right or wrong, nor do they make them good or bad. They just don't fit in *your* company culture. If they go somewhere that has their values, they'll be fine and they'll probably thrive. Keeping in mind your core values, it's now time to turn to the tool that will show you what you have.

THE PEOPLE ANALYZER

I often observed my clients discussing people issues in terms that were very subjective and unproductive. They often never really resolved their people issues, and when they did, the process took twice as long as it should have. Out of necessity, I created a tool to make such discussions much more tangible.

NAME	BE HUMBLY CONFIDENT	GROW OR DIE	HELP FIRST	DO THE RIGHT THING	DO WHAT YOU SAY
JOHN SMITH	+	+	+	+	+
SALLY JONES	-	-	-	-	-
GEORGE WILSON	+/-	+/-	+/-	+/-	+/-

The People Analyzer is designed to clarify whether you have the right person in place or not. This is one of the top five tools used by all my clients. The concept was actually created by my dad back in the early 1970s for evaluating salespeople, and I have altered it into a tool that helps evaluate an individual's core values. The People Analyzer template can be downloaded from **www.eosworldwide.com/people.**

First, put the names of the people you're going to analyze in the left column. Then list your core values across the top. Then rate each person according to his or her adherence to the core values. Give one of three ratings:

+ He or she exhibits that core value most of the time.

+/- Sometimes he or she exhibits the core value and
  sometimes he or she doesn't.

- He or she doesn't exhibit the core value most of the time.

You will notice in the preceding example, John is absolutely the right person for your organization, George is very much on the fence, and Sally must go.

The ideal you're shooting for in your organization is to surround yourself with 100 percent of the right people, who look just like John does. However, this is only an ideal, so don't get caught up in perfection. What your leadership team has to do is determine what the bar is. The "bar" is the minimum standard you will accept from the People Analyzer results. The power of setting the bar is that you give all managers absolute clarity on what is acceptable and what is not.

Once managers know your expectations, they will hold their people accountable accordingly.

The recommended bar for a company with five core values is three pluses, two plus/minuses, and never a minus. This is strictly my recommendation based on past experience. I have clients with higher and lower bars, so you must decide for yourself. The key point is that anyone who is at or above the bar is the right person, and your goal is to get 100 percent of the right people in your organization.

THE THREE-STRIKE RULE

What do you do if someone is below the bar? Before you make any drastic decisions, I highly recommend that you first communicate the People Analyzer results to the person and give that person the chance to better his or her performance. He or she will improve almost all of the time. The question is, will he or she improve enough to move above the bar? Most people will, some won't, but you should give them a chance to perform according to the new structure.

The three-strike rule works as follows:

Strike One: Discuss the issues and your expectations with the person, and give him or her 30 days to correct the problem.

Strike Two: If you don't see improvement, discuss his or her performance again and give him or her another 30 days.

Strike Three: If you still don't see improvement, he or she is not going to change and must go. When the termination finally happens, all of those who are the right people will thank you for it and wonder what took you so long.

In practice, you will discover that you don't have to fire people most of the time. Once you create an awareness of your core values through your initial speech, quarterly state-of-the-company meetings, the People Analyzer, performance reviews, and the three-strike rule, the people that don't fit won't last until the third strike. Some don't even last until the first. Instead, they'll leave on their own, because they know they don't fit.

What this process does is smoke them out. Consider the following example: One leadership team had a member that was definitely not a fit. He was the VP of sales and marketing. In our first two sessions, I watched him sweat through creating their Accountability Chart and squirm through the process of discovering their core values. It was becoming very clear why the company's sales had stagnated for a few years. By the third session, he begged off, saying he had an important client meeting out of town and could not attend. By the fourth session, he had quit the company and taken another position. He was then replaced with someone who was the right person in the right seat. As a result, the client experienced growth for the first time in three years. This is a perfect example of how someone can muddle through in an organization that lacks clarity over roles, values, and expectations. When these tools are in place, with increased focus and accountability, there is simply no place for them to hide.

I recommend the four following steps to use with the People Analyzer:

STEP 1
After discovering your core values as a leadership team, "people-analyze" each other, as all EOS clients do. This will accomplish two objectives. First, it will validate your core values. If you're all weak in one particular value, you should question whether or not it truly should be included. Second, you will see if someone on the leadership team is below the bar. While this tough situation does not come up often, you must follow the three-strike rule with this person as well. Most of the time, this person will improve his or her performance. Sometimes he or she will opt out.

STEP 2
Have your leadership team people-analyze everyone in the organization and then have each manager share those results in one-on-one sessions. This will bring the tool to life throughout the organization.

STEP 3
Use the People Analyzer in your quarterly performance reviews with all team members. Let them analyze you as well. Don't be afraid to put your money where your mouth is.

STEP 4

If your leadership team is struggling with a personnel problem, run the person through the People Analyzer. This will give you a clear perspective on whether it's a right-person issue. If it is, there is nothing more to discuss and you now know how to solve it. If it isn't, and it might be the person's seat, don't worry—we'll cover that next.

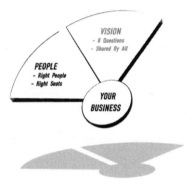

RIGHT SEATS

Once you're confident you have selected the right people, it's important to get them in the right seats. That means all of your people are operating in their Unique Abilities® and those abilities are clearly in line with their roles and responsibilities.

A seat cannot be created until the organization is structured in the right way so as to lift your company to the next level. To create that structure, we'll use a powerful tool called an Accountability Chart. This is a supercharged organizational chart, and, when completed, it will help owners and leadership team members clearly grasp their own roles and responsibilities. That will, in turn, enable them to do the same for their people.

THE ACCOUNTABILITY CHART

This tool does not assume there is only one way to structure an organization. You could read a hundred books on organizational development and find a hundred different opinions on the way to structure an organization. The key question is this: What is the right structure to move your organization forward in the next six to 12 months?

Next to the V/TO, the Accountability Chart has the most impact of any EOS tool. It forces its users to view their organization in a different way and to address people issues that have been holding them back for years.

For this exercise to have impact on your company, you'll need to instill a few ground rules:

1. You must look forward. You cannot look back or get caught up in the present. It will distort your judgment.

2. You must detach yourself from the existing business, your current role, and your ego.

3. You must elevate yourself above the business, look down on it, and make decisions for the long-term greater good of the company.

The Accountability Chart starts with a fundamental belief that there are only three major functions in any business and those three functions make every organization run, regardless of whether it's a start-up business or the largest company in the world.

To illustrate the three major functions, picture three boxes side by side by side. In the box to the left, you have the first major function: sales and marketing. In the middle box is the second: operations. In the box to the right, you have the third: finance and administration. You may call them by different names, but those are the three major functions. Sales and marketing generate business. Operations provides the service or manufactures the product, and takes care of the customer. Finance and administration manage the monies flowing in and out as well as the infrastructure.

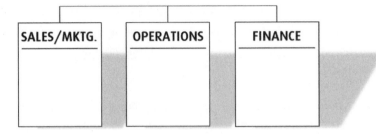

Assuming that three major functions exist in all organizations, the next truth is that they must all be strong.

I've had many debates about whether sales and marketing is the most important function. The argument is always that until somebody sells something, nothing else happens. That's hard to disagree with. But realistically, all three have to be strong.

To make the point, let's consider three scenarios:

- You have a strong sales and marketing function, a weak operations function, and a strong financial function. What's the net effect? In that scenario, you're doing a great job selling and bringing in new customers, but you're losing them right out the back because operations is not delivering what you promised and customers aren't happy.

- You have a strong sales and marketing function, a strong operations function, and a weak financial function. What's the net effect? Again, you'll bring in a lot of customers and take good care of them, but money is coming in the front door and going right out the back due to a lack of financial controls: $10 million in and $10 million out, or worse, $10 million in and $10.2 million out. This may strike a nerve because many companies fall into a situation where there is no monitoring of spending, nor is individual customer profitability assessed.

- You have a weak sales and marketing function, a strong operations function, and a strong financial function. What's the net effect? A bunch of talented people in operations and finance are waiting around for something to happen, and nothing is.

If any of the three major functions are weak, your organization is not as effective. Given that they are all equally important, it's time to apply the Accountability Chart. In order to maintain accountability, only one person can ultimately be in charge of any major function within an organization. Only one person oversees sales and marketing, only one person runs operations, and only one person manages finance and administration. When more than one person is accountable, nobody is.

When leadership teams do this exercise for the first time, they often discover they have two or even three names in a box. This may happen with you as well. If it does, you've uncovered a root issue for your company's lack of growth or chaos, and you must solve it by reducing the number of names to one. The all-for-one and one-for-all approach won't build a solid company. It may have gotten you here, but only clear accountability will boost you to the next level.

To take structure a step further, these three functions cannot operate independently of each other. That's why all great organizations have another major function, a role that I like to call the integrator.

INTEGRATORS
The integrator is the person who harmoniously integrates the major functions of the business. When those major functions are strong and you have strong people accountable for each, great healthy friction and tension will occur between them. The integrator blends that friction into greater energy for the company as a whole.

I use the term "integrator" to cut through all the wonderful titles for this role, such as CEO, president, general manager, king, or queen. It doesn't matter what you call it, but the bottom line is that the integrator is the person who has the Unique Ability® to run the organization, manage day-to-day issues that arise, and integrate the three major functions. The integrator is the glue that holds the company together.

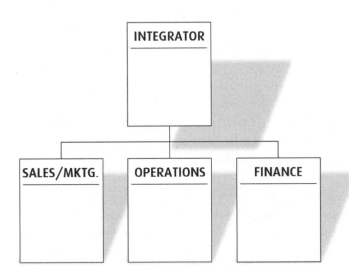

That is the basic structure of the Accountability Chart. With that understanding, two other very important factors need to be taken into account when creating the right structure for your organization.

First of all, when customizing the Accountability Chart for your company, the three major functions might split into more functions. For example, sales and marketing sometimes splits into a distinct sales function and a distinct marketing function. Operations sometimes splits into two or three distinct functions such as delivery, project management, or customer service. Finance and administration can split into as many as four: finance, administration, information technology (IT), and human resources (HR).

Depending on the size and state of your organization, you will end up with anywhere between three and ten major functions on that front line. As long as you stay focused on what the right structure is for your organization, the right number will come. Please remember, though, less is more. Not one EOS client has more than seven major functions.

The second factor is another major function that is not on the front line. In my experience, when a company creates its Accountability Chart, half the time they realize that besides an integrator integrating the major functions, there's another very powerful role in the organization. This role shows up above the integrator function, and it's called the visionary.

VISIONARIES

The concept of the visionary within an Accountability Chart is one of my greatest discoveries. I've had clients teach this concept at universities to MBAs on my behalf. Understanding and implementing this concept is eye-opening and empowering. Frankly, it has also kept some partners from killing each other.

The visionary and the integrator couldn't be more different. In a small to mid-size company, the visionary is typically the owner, co-owner, or founder. In a partnership, most of the time, one partner is the visionary and the other is the integrator. It's a dynamic that has elevated them to where they are. The visionary typically has 10 new ideas a week. Nine of them might not be so great, but one usually is, and it's that one idea each week that keeps the organization growing. For this reason, visionaries are invaluable. They're typically very creative. They're great solvers of big ugly problems (not the little practical ones), and fantastic with important clients, vendors, suppliers, and banking relationships. The culture of the organization is very important to them, because they usually operate more on emotion and therefore have a better barometer of how people are feeling. If you're one, know thyself and be *free*.

By contrast, integrators are typically very good at leading, managing, and holding people accountable. They love running the day-to-day aspects of the business. They are accountable for profit and loss, plus the overall business plan for the organization. They remove obstacles so that people running the major functions can execute. They're great at special projects. In sum, they operate more on logic. If you are one, know thyself and be *stressed*.

One University of California professor lectures that you always need both an entrepreneur and a manager at the top of a company. An entrepreneur's lust needs to be counterbalanced with a manager's prudence and discipline. He is making the same point as the visionary/integrator relationship, just using different terminology. When it's structured correctly, the dynamic that exists between the two Unique Abilities® can be magical.

For a deeper dive into the visionary/integrator dynamic, read *Rocket Fuel: The One Essential Combination That Will Get You More of What You Want from Your Business*. Written with my co-author, Mark C. Winters, it is a complete how-to manual for finding, developing, and maximizing your visionary/integrator relationship.

When Asphalt Specialists, Inc. (ASI), a paving company with annual revenues of $40 million and 120 employees, began The EOS Process, their leadership team was dysfunctional and they had just suffered their first ever unprofitable year. The two owners, brothers Bruce and Dan, were not seeing eye to eye. They were corunning the company, and neither was in the right seat. Dan was entrenched in all aspects of the business and quickly burning out, while Bruce was selling full-time and becoming very frustrated with the state of things.

The creation of their Accountability Chart led to an understanding of the visionary and integrator roles. Through realizing their true skill sets, the two brothers clearly defined their seats. Bruce is now the visionary and Dan is the integrator. With a clear vision, their leadership team is now healthy and eager to accomplish their goal of becoming the best-quality asphalt paving company in their market. At a time when new construction in the region was at a 20-year low and other competing asphalt companies were struggling to stay in business, last year was their most profitable ever.

My first experience with the power of the visionary/integrator roles occurred in my very first company, Wickman Productions, which my dad and I more or less co-ran. As a textbook visionary, he quickly became frustrated with the day-to-day running of the business but kept getting his hands into everything. As a textbook integrator, I wanted him to stay out of my way and let me handle the nuts and bolts.

With frustrations building on both sides, I booked a conference room at a Marriott hotel for the day. I prepared a presentation and locked us in a room. I illustrated what the visionary should do for the greater good of the organization, which was my dad's Unique Ability®, and what the integrator should do, which was mine. When all of the dust settled, we were both clearly in our right seats, with clear roles and responsibilities, motivated, and ready to go. That was another key factor in accomplishing the turnaround for the company. Clear accountability will take you to the next level.

It's common for a company to have a visionary but no integrator. This causes a real struggle, because the visionary is constantly frustrated with his or her lack of traction. In addition, he or she has to keep acting as the integrator and get pulled into the day-to-day management of the business. For instance, Bob Shenefelt is a pure visionary. He built his first organization, Great White, to $10 million in revenue and then successfully sold it. He made the *Inc.* 500 fastest-growing companies list, had a thriving culture, and—guess what? He also had a partner who was an integrator.

In his second company, RCS, he struggled to gain traction and grow past $4 million over a four-year period because he hadn't found the right integrator. Last year, Bob brought on the right integrator—Patrick Gysel—to fill the role. RCS grew 40 percent, and this year, it will achieve revenues of at least $7 million with no end to further growth in sight.

What makes the Accountability Chart more than just an organizational chart is that once the major functions are clear, each is defined by five major roles. As an example, the visionary function's five roles might be as follows:

- R&D/ideas
- Creative problem-solving
- Major relationships
- Culture
- Selling

The chart on the following page shows the most common examples of the five major roles for each major function. Remember that about half of all organizations have a visionary role, and the others don't. This is represented by the dotted line around the visionary.

LMA stands for *leading, managing,* and holding people *accountable.* Anyone in the Accountability Chart who has people reporting to him or her has a vital responsibility of LMA. This requires time, energy, and Unique Ability®.

You now map out your entire organization using the Accountability Chart structure. Illustrate all of the functions in your organization and which function they report to, and then list the five major roles of that function. Determine if you have a visionary in your organization. If you do, illustrate it clearly.

As you construct your Accountability Chart, a few words of caution: Create only the structure first. Don't put any names in any of the boxes yet. In other words, illustrate the correct functions at all levels in the organization. This method will keep you honest with yourself and lead you to the best structure. Once the right structure is set, then put the right people in the right seats. When you choose someone for that seat, you want to be certain that person is operating in his or her Unique Ability®.

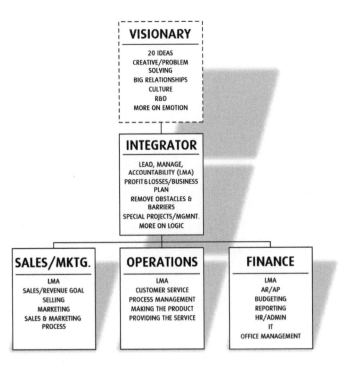

When you're finished, the Accountability Chart should look like an organizational chart, with five bullets that illustrate the major roles of each function. Important note: The Accountability Chart will clarify function, role, and reporting structure, but it will not define communication structure. Your communication should flow freely across all lines and departments where necessary, creating an open and honest culture. With each position's accountability clear and communication crossing all departments, you will avoid cross-departmental issues. The Accountability Chart should in no way create silos or divisions.

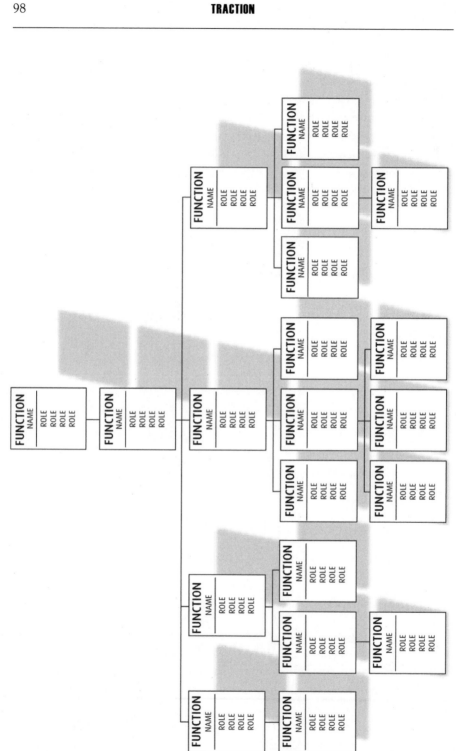

YOUR LEADERSHIP TEAM

With the completion of your Accountability Chart, the visionary, if you have one, the integrator, and the people heading up the major functions will become your leadership team. You now have representation and accountability for all the major functions of the business. Now that your leadership team is clearly in place, the next four chapters will address how you meet, prioritize, communicate, report, solve issues, and execute your vision.

GWC

Your completed Accountability Chart clarifies who is accountable for what. With this level of clarity, it's time to put all the right people into the right seats. To do that you need only one filter: GWC.

GWC stands for *get it, want it*, and *capacity* to do it. GWC is a tool that stemmed from thousands of hours of working with leaders. The concept crystallized for me while sitting in a coffee shop with a client. We were discussing why one of his moves, that of elevating one of his key people to the role of integrator, hadn't yet borne fruit. He had the right person, but the promotion hadn't worked. At that moment, the answer to a question that had been bothering me clicked into place. After hundreds of sessions, I suddenly understood why filling seats hadn't worked for some. I explained the concept of GWC to him. As a result of the clarity GWC gave him, he immediately realized he had made a wrong-seat mistake. The person who got the job had wanted it, but didn't have the capacity to do it. That person was promptly removed from the role and put in a more suitable position, where he now excels.

The discovery came after observing many who'd been given seats but did not step up and fully assume their roles. These people were not fully performing because one of the three factors was absent. They didn't get it, didn't want it, or didn't have the capacity to do the job.

To reach the next level, you need the people that report to you to be able to take the ball and run with it. When you as their leader or manager clearly articulate the seat (including roles, responsibilities, expectations, and measurables) and present that opportunity, you have created an opening. One of two things will happen as a result: Either they will step up and take charge, or they never will. If they don't, it's because one of G, W, or C is missing. In this scenario, you'll be frustrated, they'll be frustrated, you'll never be able to delegate and elevate, and you'll always be forced to do some or all of their work. Let's break down these assets one at a time.

Get It

You've seen people who get it and people who don't. "Get it" simply means that they truly understand their role, the culture, the systems, the pace, and how the job comes together. Not everyone gets it. The good news is that there are plenty who do.

Want It

This means they genuinely like the job. They understand the role, and they want to do it based on fair compensation and the responsibility. In many instances, a manager feels the need to motivate, overpay, or beg a person to want it, when the reality is they don't. Sometimes their ego, your hopes, or their ignorance about what the job entails will lead them to think that they want it. But if they don't, they're never going to provide that spark, no matter how effective a manager you are. So stop beating your head against the wall. Find someone who does want it, and the difference will be immediately apparent.

Capacity to Do It

Capacity means having the time as well as the mental, physical, and emotional capacity to do a job well. Sometimes, a position might require a commitment of 55 hours a week where the person is only willing to commit 40. Sometimes the job requires a certain level of intellect, skill, knowledge, and emotional intelligence, and the person doesn't have that capacity. This is the Peter Principle at its finest, where people are elevated to a level of incompetence.

A "no" on any of these three means it's not the right seat for the person, it's not their Unique Ability®. You must not fool yourself on this point. You can occasionally turn a "no" into a "yes" if you're willing to invest the time and money it takes to elevate a person. However, in most cases, you won't have the time to wait for them to adjust to the learning curve.

Be careful not to assume you already have people to fill the major functions. Just because they currently have the job doesn't always mean that they get it, want it, and have the capacity. Using the filter of GWC will keep you honest with yourself.

When Ronnisch Construction Group, a general contractor with revenues of $44 million and 37 employees, started the process, Bernie Ronnisch, the owner and integrator, had a leadership team of four. As an unbiased party, I can tell when someone is not going to cut it on the leadership team very early on, usually well before the integrator sees it. In this case, two out of the four members were not going to make it—that's 50 percent of the team! We struggled through the tasks of setting quarterly priorities, creating the Accountability Chart, and discovering core values, and then went through several quarters of poor completion on achieving those priorities. In a fit of frustration, I asked the two members directly how committed they were to this process on a scale of 1 to 10. They both gave a 4.

That was all Bernie had to hear to make some tough changes. Though both were very talented, he removed them from the leadership team. One he let go, and the other was moved to a superintendent role and shortly thereafter quit. Bernie replaced them with the right people in the right seats. Eighteen months later, the company grew 50 percent in that calendar year. Once a solid leadership team of five (Bernie added a major function) was firmly in place, they went to work on the rest of the company. Painfully they turned over 40 percent of their employees. As a result, they now have the right people in the right seats organization-wide. Four years after starting The EOS Process, their growth of 70 percent last year put them seventh on the *Crain's Detroit Business* list of fastest-growing companies. They were also a finalist for the Ernst & Young Entrepreneur of the Year award.

I've been tracking a statistic over the last 11 years regarding my client leadership team changes in their first two years of implementing EOS. The data shows that 80 percent of the time, there's a change in the leadership team as a result of this process. This means that most of the time, the leadership team that you start with is not the one you will end up with. Half the time, the change is removing someone from the team, and half the time, it's adding someone to the team. The point is this: If you're truly going to commit to building a great company, a strong leadership team, and getting the right people in the right seats, you must prepare for change on your leadership team. However, you may be one of the 20 percent in which there is no change.

Life is much easier for everyone when you have people around you who genuinely get it, want it, and have the capacity to do it.

With GWC now clear, incorporate it into your People Analyzer. When you're evaluating your people, the rating on GWC should be a black-and-white "yes" or "no," unlike the pluses and minuses for core values. You must get a "yes" on all three, or the person is in the wrong seat.

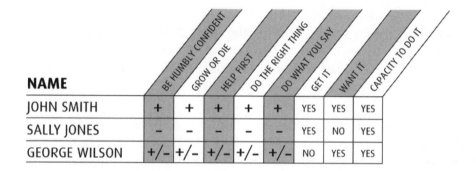

NAME	BE HUMBLY CONFIDENT	GROW OR DIE	HELP FIRST	DO THE RIGHT THING	DO WHAT YOU SAY	GET IT	WANT IT	CAPACITY TO DO IT
JOHN SMITH	+	+	+	+	+	YES	YES	YES
SALLY JONES	–	–	–	–	–	YES	NO	YES
GEORGE WILSON	+/–	+/–	+/–	+/–	+/–	NO	YES	YES

ONE NAME, TWO SEATS

You can have one name in two seats, just not two names in one seat. When an organization first starts out, the founding entrepreneur occupies every seat. He or she is the one name in all seats. He or she is the integrator, the head of sales and marketing, the head of operations, and the head of finance. As the organization grows, new people are brought in to fill the seats needed. For instance, once the entrepreneur reaches capacity, he or she then brings in someone to run operations and is able to let go of that major function.

If you're at a point where you have people in more than one seat—for instance, your bookkeeper is also your shipping person and your customer service person—that is okay, as long they have enough time to do both jobs well. It's a matter of the size of the organization. If they or you don't have enough time to be in all seats, that will have to change. This leads us to the next point.

DELEGATE AND ELEVATE

As your company grows, you have to rise to your Unique Ability®, and the same goes for your leadership team. With your Accountability Chart in place, you can now determine when someone is working at full capacity. Each person only has 100 percent of his or her working time. This 100 percent represents the amount of time each person is willing to work and still maintain balance. For some people, it's 40 hours per week, and for others, it's 70 hours. Everyone is different.

When the amount of work requires more than 100 percent to do the job well, say 120 percent, something has to give. This person needs to delegate and elevate the extra 20 percent because he or she is holding the organization back and hitting the ceiling. In some cases, it's time to move this person into one seat rather than the two he or she is occupying right now. If this person is in one seat, he or she needs to delegate more to other people, realize some efficiency, or eliminate some tasks altogether. At all times, you want to make sure that this person is drawing closer and closer to his or her Unique Ability®.

For example, assume you have a great operations and a great finance person in place, freeing you up from those major functions. Yet your workload is still requiring 120 percent of your time in order to lead and manage your leadership team as the integrator, manage the sales team, sell, and create marketing materials. It's time to let go of something else. Assuming that leading and managing the leadership team and selling are your Unique Abilities®, you must delegate managing the sales team and creating marketing materials to free up the 20 percent. Delegate to the right person in the right seat and elevate yourself to your Unique Ability®.

When you delegate and elevate, it's vital that you have the right person in the right seat. If you don't, you'll never feel completely comfortable letting go. You must also realize that you have no choice but to delegate. If you're at 120 percent, you're holding the organization back and probably starting to burn out. You no longer have the time to fully run the company and manage the sales team well—never mind those other jobs. If the only reason you're not letting go is because of the person occupying the seat, it's time to make that tough decision. You can't keep doing this person's work for him or her. You can't keep taking on his or her "monkeys," as Hal Burrows, William Oncken, Jr., and Kenneth Blanchard illustrated so well in their book, *The One Minute Manager Meets the Monkey*.

Envision all of your direct reports' responsibilities, problems, and issues as monkeys. When your direct report walks into your office with a problem, he or she is trying to leave his or her monkey with you. At the end of the day, after multiple people have walked into your office with their problems and left them with you, you end up with 20 monkeys jumping around your office. If someone walks in with a monkey, he or she needs to walk out with it. If he or she can't or won't, you've hired the wrong person.

Tyler Smith of Niche Retail is a textbook example of someone who has been able to constantly delegate and elevate as his organization has grown and continuously broken through new ceilings. When Tyler and his partner, Brad Sorock, started their Internet retail company (with Tyler as integrator and Brad as visionary), Tyler handled all sales, operations, and finance, while Brad was in the lab researching and finding the next product idea and strategy. Tyler would get a ping on his cell phone indicating he had received an order, and he would go down to his basement and print the order, package it, and ship it out. He would then process the payment, order from his supplier, and pay the bills. This went on for the first year.

As the business grew, he reached full capacity. He couldn't do all of his former jobs anymore. His first delegation and elevation was to his wife, Stacey, who helped him pack boxes. Soon, they reached capacity again. He hired someone to help him ship orders, and he let go of that function completely. He then moved to a 2,000-square-foot warehouse that could handle all of the inventory, which created the need for an operations manager. He then hired a bookkeeper and let go of that function. The growth continued.

Niche moved to a 10,000-square-foot warehouse. That created the need for a CFO and then a COO, as well as a head of site stores and marketing. Further growth required an 80,000-square-foot warehouse, and the story continues to this day. Tyler masterfully delegated and elevated each time he reached capacity, avoiding burnout. In addition, each member of the leadership team continues to delegate and elevate as the organization continues to grow. Here is Niche Retail's evolving Accountability Chart:

Year 1
4 People/$500K Revenue

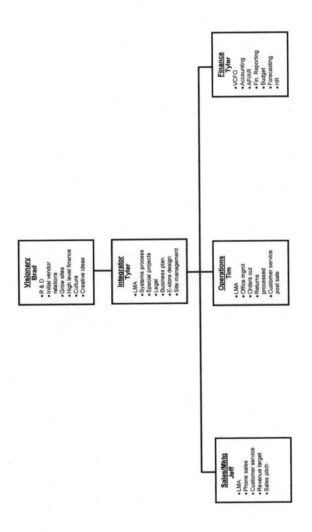

Year 2
15 People/$2.1M Revenue

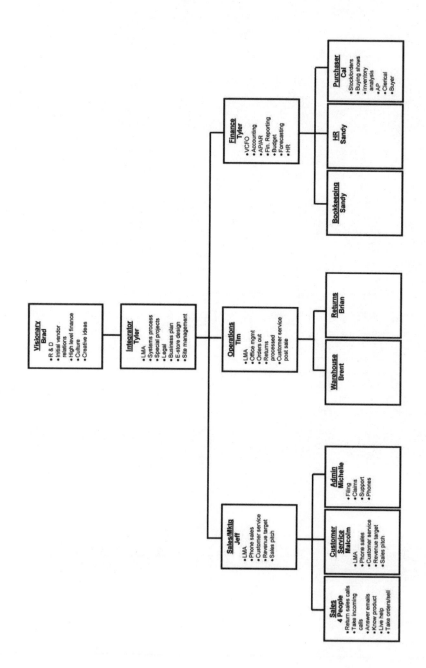

Year 3
26 People/$6M Revenue

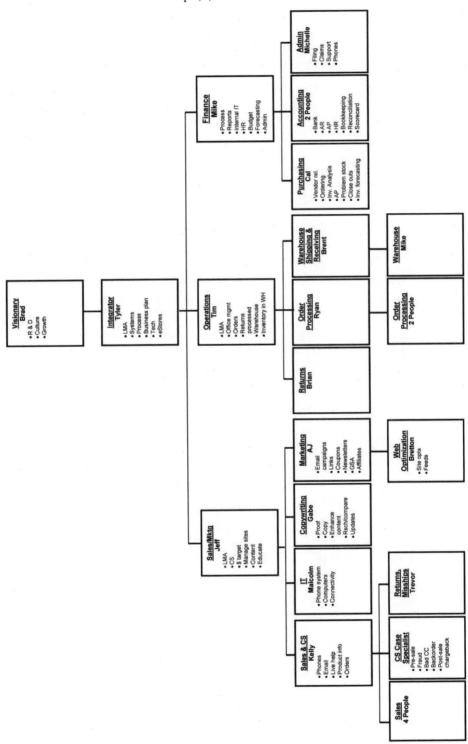

Year 5
43 People/$14.1M Revenue

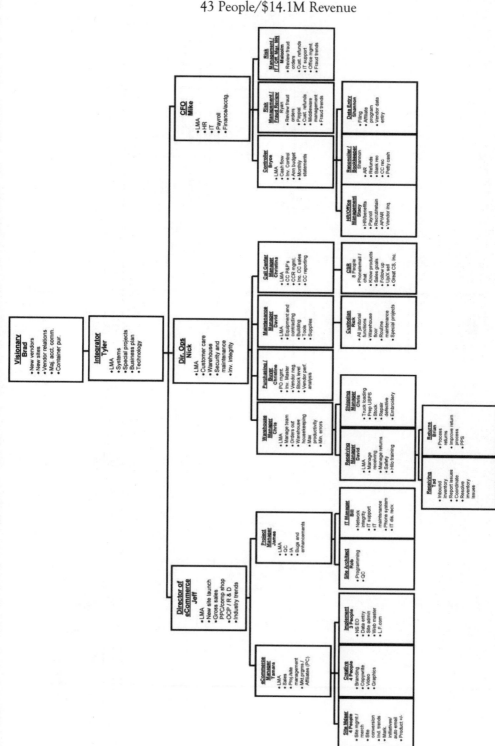

EVOLUTION

As your organization grows, your Accountability Chart will constantly evolve and change, as you can see in the example on the preceding pages featuring Niche Retail. This is a dynamic tool. Think back to what your structure looked like when you were half your size. Now imagine what it would look like at double the size. What are the differences? The point is that the Accountability Chart is an ever-evolving tool if you're growing. At a growth rate of 20 percent, you will make a change to the Accountability Chart about every 90 days.

SCALABILITY

When you build out your Accountability Chart, you will notice that certain functions require multiple people doing the same job (e.g., salespeople, customer service representatives, accounting clerks). The Accountability Chart becomes scalable. Where multiple people have the same job, you simply put the number of people in that function rather than adding multiple new boxes.

For example, if you look at Niche Retail's Year 5 Accountability Chart under the call center manager, you'll see the customer service representative (CSR) function with eight people in it.

YOUR EXISTING ORGANIZATIONAL CHART

You may be wondering what to do with your existing organizational chart. Your newly created Accountability Chart should replace it and become the tool you use to illustrate the organizational structure. It clearly shows the reporting structure and the roles and responsibilities of each function. Keep it simple. The next step is to share it with everyone in your company. They'll appreciate knowing where they fit and what they are accountable for.

From there, assuming they have your core values and GWC, let go of the vine and let them execute. You will experience the incredible results that come from harnessing all of their combined talents.

TERMINATIONS

A word of caution: Now that you've created clarity, you'll clearly see the people that do not fit in the organization. Yet you shouldn't run out and fire them all. That would make you vulnerable as an organization and leave some gaping holes.

Take a methodical approach to personnel changes, making sure that everyone on the leadership team is on the same page and then moving forward step by step. This doesn't give you an out. It just means that you can't put the company in a vulnerable position. You still have to make the change.

Once, my parents went out of town at a time when my two teenage brothers and I still lived at home. Upon their return, my dad realized we hadn't watered my mom's plant and it was quickly dying. We decided that overwatering it would do the trick, and of course it didn't. Upon noticing the problem, my mom simply grabbed a pair of scissors and pruned a few dying limbs. The plant came back to life a short time later.

You must do a little pruning from time to time for the organization to flourish. Merely hoping that poorly fitting people will make it, sending them to a seminar, or giving them a pep talk is like overwatering the plant. It isn't going to solve the problem. Once you do the necessary pruning, your organization will be revitalized.

36 HOURS OF PAIN

If people must go, and you're procrastinating because the prospect of firing them seems painful, hopefully this will give you some motivation. During the evolution of Niche Retail illustrated on the previous pages, Tyler Smith kept someone around for a year too long because he was having a really hard time making the decision to let the person go. What made it equally tough was this person had been with them through the early years. The company outgrew him, though. He was aware of this, and over time, his attitude had soured. The leadership team finally pulled out the People Analyzer and the results showed there was simply no other option. The person was no longer right for the organization. As a result, after much anguish and soul-searching Tyler finally made the tough decision to let him go. A couple of days later, Tyler called me and shared a term that is now an EOS staple: 36 hours of pain.

The hours leading up to and including the termination were painful, but after that point, he realized it was one of the best decisions he had made for the greater good of the company. He couldn't understand why he hadn't done it sooner. The work environment was so much better and less tense for everyone. He was relieved.

Other employees thanked him for making the tough decision. He experienced all that pain for a year, when in hindsight he could have experienced only 36 hours of pain, probably for both parties. Incidentally, the terminated gentleman is now doing well and pursuing his passion. The decision was best for all.

If the People Analyzer shows you that someone is the wrong person for your organization, make the decision. And yes, there will be some pain, but only for about 36 hours.

Keep two important points in mind:

1. Be careful what you wish for because you'll get it. If you want to grow, you have to understand that not everyone is going to be able to keep up and remain in the same seat forever.

2. Keeping people around just because you like them is destructive. You're doing a disservice to the company, to everyone in it, and to the person. People must add value. I realize this may sound cold, but to the degree people are in the right seats, everyone is happier, especially them.

THE THREE QUESTIONS TO ASK
When a client completes its Accountability Chart, we ask three questions to confirm that it is at 100 percent. Please ask these three questions with your leadership team:

1. Is this the right structure to get us to the next level?

2. Are all of the right people in the right seats?

3. Does everyone have enough time to do the job well?

A "yes" on all three confirms that you're at 100 percent in this essential component.

We now know what great leaders mean when they attribute their success to surrounding themselves with good people. It's putting the right people (core values) in the right seats (GWC and Unique Ability®).

With your vision clear and shared by all, and with the right people in the right seats, the next step is measuring your progress and having an absolute pulse on your business. That requires the use of data.

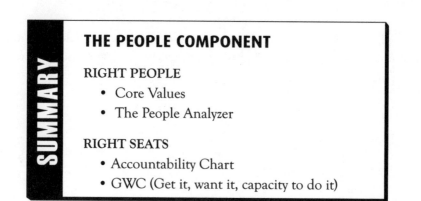

THE PEOPLE COMPONENT

RIGHT PEOPLE
- Core Values
- The People Analyzer

RIGHT SEATS
- Accountability Chart
- GWC (Get it, want it, capacity to do it)

CHAPTER 5

THE
DATA COMPONENT

SAFETY IN NUMBERS

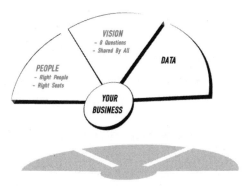

Picture a small plane flying over the Atlantic Ocean. Halfway across, the captain announces, "I've got bad news and I've got good news. The bad news is that the gauges aren't working. We are hopelessly lost, I have no idea how fast we're flying or in what direction, and I don't know how much fuel we have left. The good news is that we're making great time!"

Does that sound at all familiar? That's how most entrepreneurs run their organizations. They're flying blind with no data to let them gauge where they are, where they are going, or if they are heading in the right direction. But they always remain optimistic.

Doubts can eat away at you. If you're a typical business owner, you often wake up at 2:00 a.m. with an uneasy feeling. You feel you can't accurately measure the pulse of your business. To take that pulse, you walk around the office the next day and talk to five different people. In the process, you waste a lot of your time and other people's, and after all that talking, what you have are subjective opinions, not hard data. Only factual information can provide the basis for productive discussion and decision-making.

This chapter is designed to help you formulate and manage your data to let you take the pulse of your business consistently and accurately so that you can then take effective action. You will no longer be managing assumptions, subjective opinions, emotions, and egos.

You will gain the power of being able to manage your business through a chosen handful of numbers. These numbers will allow you to monitor your business on a weekly basis, quickly showing which activities are on track or off track. Once you have tracked those numbers for a while, you will achieve the valuable ability to see patterns and trends to predict the future.

For the Data Component, you will be introduced to a time-tested tool that will allow you to quantify your company's results. It's called a Scorecard, and once you learn to use it, you'll be able to accurately read the pulse of your business. With hard data in hand, you'll sleep better at night. Ultimately, you will have the ability to let go of the vine and be better connected than ever. In addition, you will reach the point where everyone in your organization has a number, a meaningful, manageable measurable. This will give them clear direction and increase productivity.

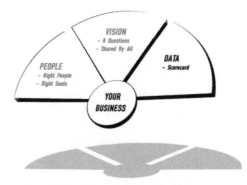

SCORECARD

According to an old business maxim, anything that is measured and watched is improved. The concept of managing through a Scorecard has been around for a long time. The idea has been expressed through many different terms. It's been called a dashboard, flash report, scoreboard metrics, measurables, key performance indicators, smart numbers, and so on. Whatever you call it, it's a handful of numbers that can tell you at a glance how your business is doing.

The unfortunate reality is that most organizations don't have a Scorecard. They lack activity-based numbers to review on a regular basis. They might rely on a

P&L (profit and loss statement) to tell them the score, but by then it's too late to make corrections. A profit and loss statement is a trailing indicator. Its data comes after the fact, and you can't change the past. With a Scorecard, however, you can change the future.

Let's look at someone who managed the most seemingly unmanageable beast of all using a Scorecard. In his book, *Leadership*, Rudolph Giuliani says in a chapter aptly titled "Everyone's Accountable, All of the Time" that one of the first things he did when he took over as mayor of New York City was to introduce CompStat. CompStat is a multilevel management tool that allows officers of the New York Police Department (NYPD) to report specific crime numbers on a daily or weekly basis.

Giuliani says it enabled local precinct commanders to see patterns and trends, and then to react and deploy officers where necessary. In the past, the NYPD had merely tracked the number of arrests and the response times to 911 calls, but these are trailing indicators. By the time these numbers were received, quarterly or even annually, the pattern of crime would have changed. CompStat tracked crime activity on a daily and weekly basis, which Giuliani says allowed the NYPD to take the pulse of crime activity and thus gain the ability to prevent crime rather than just report it.

In eight years, murder figures went down by almost 70 percent and overall crime went down by about 65 percent. In 1996, CompStat won the Innovations in Government Award from the Kennedy School of Government at Harvard University. Now many cities are using the same type of tool. After the success of CompStat, Giuliani went on to unveil a citywide Scorecard called CapStat, which allows a detailed performance evaluation of 20 city agencies.

My business mentor, Sam Cupp, showed me how he used his Scorecard to take the pulse of his companies, which totaled over $300 million in sales. In his teachings, he forced me to do the same with my business.

In my first business, I was able to manage the entire company using 14 numbers. How many numbers you need to track depends on the type of business you have. Every company's Scorecard is different. With over 400 EOS clients, there are over 400 different Scorecards. Your Scorecard will be unique to you and your organization. The following exercise will show you a step-by-step process for creating a Scorecard that fits your unique business.

STEP 1
Spend an hour with your leadership team. Imagine you're on a desert island somewhere. None of you can talk to anyone, access e-mail, or talk on the phone. All you have is a piece of paper with a handful of numbers on it. These numbers must allow you to have an absolute pulse on your business. What are all of the numbers that must be on that piece of paper? Decide and list all of the categories that you'd need to track on a weekly basis to have that pulse.

These categories should include items such as weekly revenue, cash balances, weekly sales activity, customer satisfaction/problems, accounts receivable and payable, and client project or production status, to name a few.

COMPANY SCORECARD

WHO	MEASURABLES	GOAL	JANUARY 5	12	19	26	FEBRUARY 2	9	16	23	MARCH 2	9	16	23	30
	WEEKLY REVENUE														
	CASH BALANCE														
	SALES CALLS														
	SALES MEETINGS														
	PROPOSALS														
	CLOSED BUSINESS														
	PAYROLL														
	CUSTOMER PROBLEMS														
	CUSTOMER RATING														
	ACCOUNTS RECEIVABLE														
	ACCOUNTS PAYABLE														

As a rule of thumb, you should end up with five to 15 numbers—hopefully closer to five. There is such a thing as too much information, so keep it simple. Once you've identified all the categories, you then plug them into your Scorecard template. On the previous page is a sample template in a spreadsheet format. As you can see, you list the categories under the Category heading:

STEP 2
In the left-hand column, list who is accountable for each of the numbers. Only one person is ultimately accountable for each, and it's usually the person heading up that major function. This is the person who must deliver that weekly number to the organization, not the person who simply enters the number. For example, the head of sales and marketing is accountable for hitting the sales-activity numbers, not the finance person who fills out the Scorecard each week.

STEP 3
Decide and fill in what the expected goal is for the week in each category. Now that your V/TO and vision are clear, the goal numbers in your Scorecard should be tied directly to your one-year plan.

STEP 4
Put next week's date in the first date column in preparation for filling in your Scorecard next week.

STEP 5
Decide who is accountable for collecting the numbers and fill in the Scorecard every week for the leadership to review. Decide how that person will receive the numbers from each member.

STEP 6
Use it! You must review your Scorecard every week to ensure that you're on track for your vision. The real magic of using a Scorecard is not limited to managing it on a weekly basis. You will soon see 13 weeks (three months) at a glance, which enables you to see patterns and trends. From there the numbers roll, meaning that the first week will drop off the Scorecard as the 14th week is added. Make sure you keep the numbers that drop off for future reference and historical data.

THREE SCORECARD RULES OF THUMB

1. The numbers in the Scorecard should be weekly activity-based numbers, not the type of high-level numbers you see in a profit and loss statement (P&L). Remember, this Scorecard is not a P&L. It's based on numbers showing activity and telling you whether you're on track for a strong P&L. In other words, your Scorecard *predicts* your P&L. What are activity-based numbers? To help clarify, let's look at a couple of examples.

   One category would be new revenue/sales. If you only monitor revenue as it comes in, you'll react to downslides too late. Look at your sales process and follow the steps as far back as you can. Typically you'll find that each step can be measured with a number. Take them in order, starting with the first step. Measure the number of the leads generated, the number of contacts, the number of appointments scheduled, the number of appointments attended, the number of proposals, and/or the number of closes. You decide how far back you want to measure because you can chase the process all the way back to the first step.

   Say, for instance, you choose number of new leads generated and track that number in the Scorecard. By knowing the number of leads you have, you can see how many of the leads turn into contacts, how many contacts turn into appointments, and so on. By understanding these formulas and these ratios, you'll be able to predict the number of closes two, three, and sometimes four months down the road. This ultimately gives you the ability to predict and tells you how many leads you need to develop today.

   Another example of activity-based numbers is client satisfaction. If you merely track customer complaints or lost customers, that's too late as well. Instead, go to the first step in the process—finding out what factors drive both happy and unhappy customers. For instance, you might do a proactive numerical survey, such as asking three questions that require a number-based answer every time you close the business or deliver the product. As a result, you'll create leading indicators that allow you to track how you're doing. For instance, if, on average, you receive an 8.5 rating out of 10 in a certain area of your delivery and suddenly see an average rating of 7 for a series of three weeks, you know that a problem is brewing somewhere. You then have the opportunity to solve it before you potentially lose the customer.

2. The Scorecard is much more of a proactive tool, helping you to anticipate problems before they actually happen. However, you still need to look at either monthly or quarterly financial statements and monitor a budget on a monthly or quarterly basis.

3. When managing a Scorecard, many clients find value in red-flagging categories that are off track. Red-flagging occurs when one of your numbers does not hit or exceed the goal for the week. Shade that number so it stands out in the Scorecard, usually using the color red. This can be programmed in an electronic spreadsheet or done manually. This creates better focus and awareness on that number, which creates more urgency in the weekly meeting.

Your Scorecard will evolve over the next several months. Assuming you've taken a good first cut, your categories should be about 85 percent right. That is close enough at this point. As your Scorecard is brought to life in the succeeding chapters, it will evolve to 100 percent. On average, three months have to pass until it evolves into a tool you love.

The Scorecard should cause an organizational shift. Your leadership team will become more proactive at solving problems because you'll have hard data that not only points out current problems but also predicts future ones. By solving them, you're assuring them that you're on track with your vision. In order to solve a problem, you must know the source of the number in the Scorecard; therefore you can go directly to the root cause and create better accountability and clarity with your people. That leads to the second part of the Data Component.

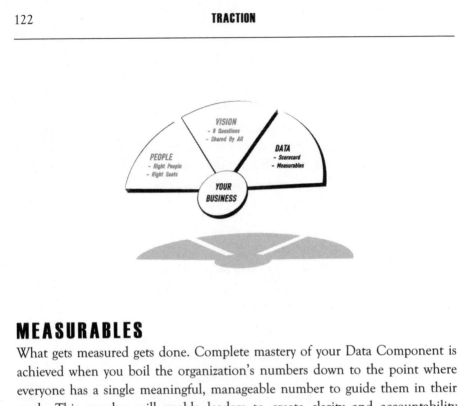

MEASURABLES

What gets measured gets done. Complete mastery of your Data Component is achieved when you boil the organization's numbers down to the point where everyone has a single meaningful, manageable number to guide them in their work. This number will enable leaders to create clarity and accountability throughout their team. With a completed Scorecard, you can track high-level numbers down to a single person as the source.

EVERYONE HAS A NUMBER

The founder and chairman of a large Michigan mortgage company and a leading online mortgage lender once gave a talk at our Entrepreneurs' Organization Chapter. This was 16 years ago, when I was running my first company and he had 75 employees. He's a fanatic about measuring everything; at one point he told us that "everyone has a number." He went on to explain how every employee in his organization has a number, even his receptionist. Hers was two, as in, "two rings good, three rings bad."

His speech was a wake-up call for me. Back at my office, I came up with and implemented a number for everyone. I have since taught this discipline to every client, and it has produced tremendous results.

Dale Carnegie's book *How to Win Friends & Influence People* contains an example illustrating the power that numbers can generate among your people: Charles Schwab ran Bethlehem Steel Company in the early 1900s, and he had a mill manager whose people weren't producing their work quota. One day Schwab asked him, "How is it that a manager as capable as you can't make this mill turn out what it should?" The mill manager didn't have an answer. He had tried everything. This conversation took place at the end of the day, just before the night shift came on. Schwab asked the manager for a piece of chalk and asked the nearest man how many heats (i.e., batches of refined steel) his shift had made that day. The man said six. Without another word, Schwab chalked a big figure six on the floor and walked away.

When the night shift came in, they saw the six and asked what it meant. The day people explained that Charles Schwab, the big boss, has asked how many heats they'd made, and chalked the number down on the floor. The next morning, Schwab walked through the mill again, and he found the night shift had rubbed out the six and replaced it with a big seven. When the day shift reported to work that morning, they too saw the seven chalked on the floor, and decided that they would show the night shift a thing or two. The crew pitched in with enthusiasm, and when they quit that night, they left behind them an enormous 10. It wasn't soon before this mill, which had been lagging way behind in production, was turning out more work than any other plant.

That shows the power of giving everyone a number. In fact, there are eight distinct advantages to everyone having a number.

1. **Numbers cut through murky subjective communication between manager and direct reports.** As an example, where the old response between sales manager and salesperson regarding last week's sales activity was a vague "Great! Things are picking up," the new number-based answer is crystal clear: "I got three." If three is good for that company, then last week was great. If they needed to get 10, there is an issue to solve. Better to solve it now than two months from now when it shows up as poor revenue in the P&L. Numbers aren't just for the person. They become a

communication tool between manager and direct report, creating the basis of comparison, unemotional dialogue, and, ultimately, results.

2. **Numbers create accountability.** When you set a number, everyone knows what the expectation is. Accountability begins with clear expectations, and nothing is clearer than a number. For example, if in the accounting department the people's expectations are "collections," that is unclear. However, if they are supposed to keep accounts receivable days below 40, balance below $100,000, or aged receivable less than $50,000, that is a clear expectation. The people know exactly what their target is.

3. **Accountable people appreciate numbers.** Wrong people in the wrong seats usually resist measurables. Right people in the right seats love clarity. Knowing the numbers they need to hit, they enjoy being part of a culture where all are held accountable. It creates an esprit de corps with everyone pitching in to make the company a success because right people want to win.

4. **Numbers create clarity and commitment.** When an employee is clear on his or her number and agrees that he or she can achieve it, you have commitment. There is no gray area. A great example is the number Nordstrom uses with its salespeople: sales per hour. The number shows up on their paychecks and perks are tied to it. Nordstrom salespeople know exactly what their sales expectations are all the way down to an hourly basis.

5. **Numbers create competition.** Charles Schwab was able to create competition by making a target number known to all teams. Sure, they might experience some discomfort and a little stress, but there is nothing wrong with a little pressure.

6. **Numbers produce results.** Similar to the way Rudolph Giuliani helped turn a city around, you can create terrific results. If the customer service department's expectation is zero unresolved customer issues, by hitting this number, you will achieve the ultimate result of customer retention and satisfaction. Or if your customer service people are accountable for ancillary sales, and they know $1,000 in daily ancillary sales will reach the total ancillary sales goal, you'll typically hit it, or at least do better than if you don't provide this number. What gets watched improves.

7. **Numbers create teamwork.** When a team composed of the the right people in the right seats agree to a number to hit, they ask themselves "how can we hit it," creating camaraderie and peer pressure. When a team of technicians are challenged to perform their service in four hours or less collectively, they will all pull together to figure out ways to achieve that number. The ones that aren't pulling their weight and hitting the number will be called out by the other team members that are.

8. **You solve problems faster.** When an activity-based number is off track, you can attack it and solve the problem proactively, unlike with an end-result based number that shows up after it's too late to change it. In addition, the use of hard data cuts through all of the subjective and emotional opinions that create murkiness and lengthen the amount of time it takes to make the right decision.

Todd Sachse of Sachse Construction immediately saw the value of everyone having a number but struggled to persuade his leadership team to embrace the concept and understand the value as well. They assumed a backlash from the employees. He asked me to present the above advantages to them, and Todd's people have now come to embrace the idea of numbers. His superintendents achieve 15-day turnaround times on punch lists. His accounting people keep accounts receivable under 30 days. Even his receptionist opens and hands out mail in less than four hours. He attributes everyone having a number as one of the key reasons that his organization grew 50 percent the following year.

If you're still stuck, a great place to find numbers for your people is your completed Accountability Chart. Look at each of the five roles for each function. One, two, or three of those five roles can be measured by a number. For example, let's say a project manager's five major roles are as follows:

- complete projects on time
- achieve margin goal on each job
- client satisfaction
- weekly reporting in on time
- achieve quality standards

Of these five, you can measure on-time, margin, client satisfaction, and possibly quality standards.

With the tabulation of data, your organization accomplishes the third essential component of gaining traction. With the vision clear, people in place, and data being managed through a Scorecard, you're creating a transparent organization where there is nowhere to hide.

Your company is open and honest. Any obstacles that stand in the way of achieving your vision will be apparent. Your job is to now remove these barriers and solve the issues holding you back.

THE DATA COMPONENT

SCORECARD
- 5 to 15 high-level weekly numbers
- Lets you have a pulse and gives you
  the ability to predict

MEASURABLES
- Everyone has a number
  - The 8 advantages to everyone having
    a number

SUMMARY

CHAPTER 6

THE
ISSUES COMPONENT

DECIDE!

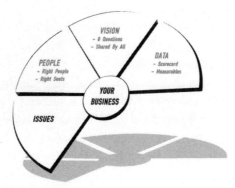

The fourth essential component of gaining traction is having the discipline to face and solve your organization's issues as they arise. When the vision is clear, the people are in place, and you're managing data, you will inevitably find out what's holding you back. Successful companies solve their issues. They don't let them linger for weeks, months, and years at a time. Problems are like mushrooms: When it's dark and rainy, they multiply. Under bright light, they diminish. In an organization where there is nowhere to hide, the problems are easily illuminated. EOS will create that strong light.

It's human nature to put off making a hard decision. If given the option, most people would prefer not to address an issue and hope that it goes away on its own. This reluctance to act can be a drag on growth and is extremely frustrating to watch. As Napoleon Bonaparte said, "Nothing is more difficult and therefore more precious than to be able to decide."

Your ability to succeed is in direct proportion to your ability to solve your problems. The better you are at solving problems, the more successful you become. This is not a new discovery. In the classic book *Think & Grow Rich*, Napoleon Hill cited a study that analyzed 25,000 people who had experienced failure. Lack of decision, or procrastination, was one of their major causes of failure. In contrast, analysis of several hundred millionaires revealed that every one of them had the habit of reaching decisions promptly and changing them slowly.

Most leadership teams spend their time discussing the heck out of everything but rarely solving anything. What is draining your energy is not having a lot of work to do; rather, it's having unresolved issues. You're about to learn a process that helps leadership teams quickly dig to the root of an issue, discuss solutions, and then decide—therefore keeping them moving forward and giving them energy by pulling up the anchors holding them back. The one statement that summarizes this chapter best is a maxim my dad taught me long ago: "It is less important what you decide than it is that you decide." More is lost by indecision than by wrong decisions.

When most new clients solve their major issues in the early stages of the process, they typically say, "That one has been around for years," or, "We've been trying to solve that issue forever." Each unresolved issue is an incomplete project weighing down your organization and holding you back. You only have so much capacity, and these unresolved issues take up time and energy. Ultimately, you or your organization will implode under the burden. By solving these issues, you'll free up capacity, creating more time and energy.

In this Issues Component chapter, you'll learn the next two EOS tools to wield against obstacles holding your company back. The first is a discipline of creating an Issues List. The second is the Issues Solving Track. Once you set them up, you'll knock those obstacles down.

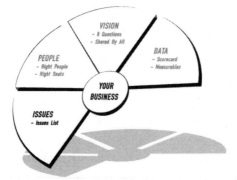

THE ISSUES LIST

It's normal to have issues. The sooner you can admit that you have them and not view that as negative thinking or some kind of a weakness, the faster you will move forward. The good news is that there are only a handful of issues in the history of business. The same ones crop up over and over again. What changes is your ability to solve them. The key is to create an environment that smokes them out.

A vital first step is creating a workplace where people feel comfortable calling out the issues that stand in the way of your vision. To do this, your leadership team must be comfortable with this type of environment. My only expectation with every EOS client is that they be open and honest with each other. To the degree that your leadership becomes open and honest, you will end up with an open and honest organization. As goes the leadership team, so goes the company. If the leadership team is open and honest, issues will flow freely.

No one has ever died from being open about issues. You have nothing to lose and everything to gain. Start with your leadership team meetings, and this behavior will trickle down throughout the entire organization. The result is an environment in which everyone feels comfortable being open and honest about everything.

If, on the other hand, the leadership team is not healthy, the organization never will be. In *The Five Dysfunctions of a Team*, Patrick Lencioni makes the point that a high level of trust is the foundation of what makes teams healthy and functional. In *Managing by Values*, authors Ken Blanchard and Michael O'Connor write that "communication happens naturally when you make the work environment safe." Trust creates an open culture in which everyone feels comfortable talking about issues as they arise.

You cannot achieve this openness if people in the organization fear losing their jobs or some other terrible ramification. Therefore, trust starts with you. You set the tone by openly admitting mistakes and issues and then working together to solve them. Everyone must know that it's okay to raise issues as long as they are corrected.

The Issues List is meaningless if no one ever puts anything useful on it. The way to get meaningful issues on the list is to create open and honest teams. When your Accountability Chart is complete, your organization will be made up by a handful of teams. Each must be healthy, starting with your leadership team. As each team becomes healthier, you will notice issues flowing more freely and the trust level increasing.

With an open and honest organization, the Issues List becomes a tool that creates a discipline to keep all of your issues out in the open and organized in one place. There should be three types of Issues Lists in your organization:

1. **The Issues List in your Vision/Traction Organizer (V/TO).** These are all company issues that can be shelved beyond 90 days. These issues are tackled in future quarterly meetings. The issues that are not a big enough priority for this week or this quarter must be stored somewhere so that you don't lose sight of them. The V/TO Issues List is the place for that. This list will include issues as diverse as new product ideas, key employee issues, technology needs, office relocation, capital needs, and the need for HR policies. They'll go there if this is not the quarter to solve them because you have bigger fish to fry.

2. **The weekly leadership team Issues List.** The time frame on these items is much shorter. These are all of the relevant issues for this week and quarter that must be tackled at the highest level. These issues will be resolved in your weekly leadership team meetings. You should not be solving departmental issues. These will typically be more strategic in nature. If it can be solved at a departmental level, push it down. Leadership issues include things as diverse as company Rocks being off track, a bad number in the Scorecard, key employee issues, major client difficulties, and process- and system-related problems.

3. **The departmental Issues List.** These issues are on a more
   local level. These include all the relevant departmental
   issues for the week that must be tackled during the weekly
   departmental meetings. The sales team might have hitting
   call numbers, presentations, closing business, marketing,
   and presentation materials on their list, while the operations
   team might have fulfilling orders, purchasing, customer
   complaints, and low production numbers on theirs.

A client shared a great idea that he used when he was having a hard time getting
the people in his department to be open and honest in the identification and
resolution of issues. For his next meeting, he made it mandatory that everyone
bring two issues. If someone did not have two, he or she could not attend
the meeting. He said it was the best meeting his team had ever had. With the
floodgates opened, they are healthier than ever.

With an open and honest culture and the three Issues Lists clear, issues will start
flowing freely. You can now compartmentalize each issue onto the appropriate
list. Each issue that arises in your organization has a place, which means you
have to start working on solving them. The most effective way to do that is by
following the Issues Solving Track.

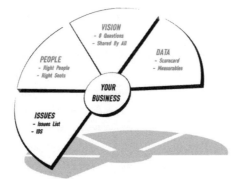

THE ISSUES SOLVING TRACK

When addressing issues, leadership teams spend most of their time discussing the heck out of everything, rarely identifying anything, and hardly ever solving something. It's truly an epidemic within the business world.

Most teams suffer from different challenges when solving issues. The common ones include fear of conflict, lack of focus, lack of discipline, lack of commitment, and personal ego. There are scores of different issue resolution models and approaches, but most people find them too complex and time-consuming. Some of the more detailed conflict resolution and problem-solving techniques require hours of preparation and mountains of paperwork. There is a better, faster, and more efficient way. After observing this phenomenon for many years, I created a simple tool that allowed my clients to resolve their issues. It's called the Issues Solving Track.

The Issues Solving Track consists of three steps:

1. Identify
2. Discuss
3. Solve

To start, you must first examine your Issues List and quickly decide on the top three issues to be solved. Do not make the mistake of starting at the top of your Issues List and working your way down. If the most important issue is seventh on the list, you will rarely handle that many issues in one sitting, and as a result you will not get to the most important one. In addition, when you take them in order of priority, a few issues will fall off the list because they turn out to be symptoms of the real issue you solved. For example, say you decide that the most important issue is that the handoff process from sales to operations is ineffective. After solving it, you might realize that the first and second issues on the list— frustration with the sales team and slow project starts—were also symptoms of the same thing. As a result, they go away on their own.

Assuming you've decided what the three most important issues are, start with the most important and follow the Issues Solving Track:

STEP 1: IDENTIFY

Clearly identify the real issue, because the stated problem is rarely the real one. The underlying issue is always a few layers down. Most of the time, the stated problem is a symptom of the real issue, so you must find the root of the matter. By batting the issue back and forth, you will reach the true cause.

Plan on getting a little bit uncomfortable. Most causes of real issues are people. The discussion can hit close to home if either someone on the leadership team or one of his or her staff is responsible. You have to be able to talk about the elephant in the room. That is why trust is so important. You have to become more vulnerable with each other and be willing to be straight about real problems. Remember the greater good.

The time spent identifying the real issue can take far longer than the time used for the second and third steps, and that's okay. That's because the root problem may have multiple symptoms. Put another way, sometimes you will spend most of your time identifying the issue. As a result, the Discuss and Solve steps will take just a few minutes because the real issue is now clear.

Here's an example. The stated issue is that John's customers are too demanding. John runs the warehouse and has been complaining that, between ordering and receiving products, customers are expecting too much with a two-day delivery time. By discussing the issue, you go from thinking that John's customers are too demanding to thinking you might not be communicating with your clients as well as you should. As you dig further, you might find that maybe the process isn't working. But through more digging, you discover that it's *John* that isn't working.

All the way down at the bottom, you realize that John is in the wrong seat. The reality is that the customer's two-day delivery request is very reasonable, and if you don't achieve it, the company will start losing those customers. John is just incapable of organizing, managing, and getting product out on time. He doesn't have the capacity (remember GWC). So, assuming you've now clearly identified the real issue—John is in the wrong seat—you can now move on to discuss what to do. Sometimes this process feels a bit like peeling an onion.

One helpful context when identifying is to understand that there are three types of issues. One is a true problem that has to be solved. The second is information that needs to be communicated and agreed to by the team. The third is an idea or opportunity that needs feedback, brainstorming, insight, and/or a green light from the team. As a result, in the identify step, it's the issue owner's responsibility to make it clear what type of issue it is and what is needed. For instance, if it's the second type of issue, the owner starts IDS by stating, "I just want to make sure that everyone is clear and agrees on the new pricing policy." This will help the entire team know the objective and makes for much more efficient issue resolution.

STEP 2: DISCUSS

Most people spend the majority of their time at this step. They rarely identify the real problem before they start discussing, and thus they rarely solve anything. They just discuss everything ad nauseam, and they actually think they are being productive.

The task of clearly identifying an issue enables you to stay focused on the issue at hand and avoid tangents. Once the issue is clearly identified, don't be afraid to suggest a solution. Sometimes you don't have to spend much time in the discussion step, because the issue is so clear and the solution is so obvious. In the above example of John, what more is there to discuss? The solution is to people-analyze John, sit down with him, determine if he can correct his issues, and then follow the three-strike rule. Taking a shot at voicing a solution forces others to react, which prompts a fuller discussion.

In its simplest form, the discussion step is everyone's opportunity to say everything they have to say about the issue. You get everything on the table in an open environment where nothing is sacred.

Everyone should say what they believe but they should say it only once, because more than once is politicking. In the discussion step, you'll need to fight for the greater good, not what is best for you or your department. If an issue is starting to hit home and the solution causes you discomfort, you must try not to push the solution in a direction that's more favorable to you or your team. If you do, you aren't fighting for the greater good of the company; you're just protecting your turf. You should have healthy conflict and let the best solution come to light, even if it causes you some pain.

Likewise, when the discussion starts to become redundant, it's time to move to Step 3. But before we do, let's have a quick word on tangents.

TANGENT ALERT!

RE/MAX First was suffering from veering off on tangents more than any other client I had ever had, so much so that I was running out of ways to help them. As a last resort, I looked up the definition of the word in the dictionary and wrote it in big block letters in front of them. When they came back from break, this is what they saw:

Tangent:
Diverging from an original purpose or course; see irrelevant

That did the trick. To this day, they are one of the best at staying focused, and are now much more productive. Incidentally, after that meeting, they went on to have their most profitable year in the history of the company.

The number one reason most leadership teams spend the majority of their time talking is tangents. I've observed teams that go on as many as 10 during the discussion of one issue. I know this because I write each of them down and then share them when the team is done discussing. That can be a great wake-up call. They'll start out talking about increasing sales, and five tangents later they're talking about letterhead. The conversation goes like this: Sales are down; we have to increase sales. Then someone brings up the salespeople and what they are doing, and from there we discuss one of the salespeople, Jack. Then the subject of Jack leads to that of Jack and Sue in accounting not getting along. This leads to the question, "Did Sue send the letter to customers who are past due?" which raises the question, "Did she use the new letterhead?"

You don't have to sit there helplessly. When someone starts to go on a tangent, get in the habit of saying "Tangent Alert!" It's a friendly triggering mechanism that keeps you on track. If the tangent is a real issue, but not relevant to the current one being discussed, put it on the Issues List and get to it in order of priority.

Upon the completion of the discussion step, all of your options, data, ideas, solutions, and concerns regarding the issue at hand will be out in the open. This enables you to move to Step 3—making the issue go away forever.

STEP 3: SOLVE

The solve step is a conclusion or solution that usually becomes an action item for someone to do. The item ends up on the To-Do List, and when the action item is completed, the issue goes away forever.

George Perles, the head football coach of the Michigan State Spartans from 1983 to 1994, once gave a dinner talk at a function I attended. He shared a mantra from his days as an assistant coach for the Pittsburgh Steelers during their heyday in the 1970s. He said, "We made every decision like we were going to the Super Bowl," and they ended up winning the Super Bowl four times. That is what every leadership team needs to do. You should make all of your decisions as though you are going to your own Super Bowl—as though you were achieving your vision.

It's important to note that you cannot jump right to solving issues without implementing the Vision Component first. If your Vision/Traction Organizer (V/TO) is not complete and your leadership isn't on the same page, you'll never solve issues well. It's like driving a car, not having a destination, and making turns randomly. If you don't know where you're going, you can't make decisions on which way to turn. Where decisions may have been difficult in the past, this step becomes much easier when your vision is clear.

Solving issues takes time. By solving issues now, you'll save time exponentially across departments by eliminating all future symptomatic issues. The old days of shoving issues to the side so you can make it to next week have to come to an end. Jury-rigging problems with duct tape and twine will become a thing of the past. To build a well-oiled machine, you have to solve issues for the long term in accordance with your vision.

Three types of resolutions will emerge from an issues-solving session. The first is when the issue is solved and requires action. For instance, "John is going to revise the accounts receivable past-due letter to include the new language." In this case, John takes the action item and completes it, and it is solved. The second is when the issue is merely awareness, and the conclusion is that everyone concurs with that awareness. For instance, "Okay, so we all agree that meetings will start on time." The third is when the issue needs more research or facts. In this case someone is assigned an action item to do the research and bring it to a subsequent meeting. For example, "Bill will gather the client data for the last two years, and we will make the issue a top priority in next week's meeting."

As you master this third step of the Issues Solving Track and become stronger at solving your own issues, your team must internalize the following 10 important aspects of solving issues.

THE 10 COMMANDMENTS OF SOLVING ISSUES
1. Thou Shalt Not Rule by Consensus
On a healthy team where the vision is clear and everyone is on the same page, eight out of 10 times, everyone will agree with the solution. However, sometimes they won't, and someone needs to make the final decision. Consensus management does not work, period. Eventually, it will put you out of business. Not everyone will be pleased in these situations, but as long as they have been heard and if the team is healthy, they can usually live with it and will support the decision. From there, you must present a united front moving forward.

One of the worst cases of consensus management was a company being run by its next generation of family members. The company's growth was stagnant, and some tough decisions needed to be made to restore profitability. In our first few sessions, every time a hard decision needed to be made, the team would either retreat out of fear of hurting someone's feelings or someone would say, "Let's vote." This had been going on for years. They were some of the nicest people you could ever meet. Yet they would come to the next session complaining about all of the same issues and how nothing was working. After a year of forcing more openness and a few very uncomfortable sessions for some people, one of the owners finally stepped up as the integrator and started to make the tough decisions. Finally, the ship is starting to turn around for them.

In countless cases of tough decisions, I've observed that in instances when the team was divided, if the integrator had gone along with the majority, it would have been the wrong decision. In a *Fortune* magazine issue on decision-making, Jim Collins is quoted as saying that in his years and years of research, "no major decision we've studied was ever taken at a point of unanimous agreement."

2. Thou Shalt Not Be a Weenie
The solution will always be simple; it's just not always easy to implement. You must have strong will, have firm resolve, and be willing to make the tough decision.

3. Thou Shalt Be Decisive
Remember the study from *Think & Grow Rich*. The 25,000 people who failed lacked the ability to make decisions and procrastinated, whereas the several hundred millionaires made decisions quickly and changed them slowly. Remember, it's less important what you decide than it is that you decide ... so, decide!

4. Thou Shalt Not Rely on Secondhand Information
You cannot solve an issue involving multiple people without all the parties present. If the issue at hand involves more than the people in the room, schedule a time when everyone can attend. Tyler Smith of Niche Retail calls these "pow-wows." When someone brings him an issue involving others or secondhand information, he says, "Time for a pow-wow" and pulls everyone involved together and solves it.

5. Thou Shalt Fight for the Greater Good
Put your egos, titles, emotions, and past beliefs aside. Focus on the vision for your organization. You will cut through the candy-coating, personalities, and politics. If you stay focused on the greater good, it will lead you to better and faster decisions.

6. Thou Shalt Not Try to Solve Them All
Take issues one at a time, in order of priority. What counts is not quantity but quality. You're never going to solve them all. The faster you understand that, the better your odds are of staying sane. Solve the most important one first, and then move on to the next.

7. Thou Shalt Live with It, End It, or Change It

This is another great lesson from my dad. In solving an issue, you have three options: You can either live with it, end it, or change it. There are no others. With this understanding, you must decide which of the three it's going to be. If you can no longer live with the issue, you have two options: Change it or end it. If you don't have the wherewithal to do those, then agree to live with it and stop complaining. Living with it should, however, be the last resort.

8. Thou Shalt Choose Short-Term Pain and Suffering

Both long-term and short-term pain require suffering. Remember the "36 hours of pain" rule, and solve your problem now rather than later.

9. Thou Shalt Enter the Danger

The issue that you fear the most is the one you most need to discuss and resolve.

10. Thou Shalt Take a Shot

Taking a shot means that you should propose a solution. Don't wait around for someone else to solve it. If you're wrong, your team will let you know. Sometimes the discussion can drag on because everyone is afraid to voice a solution even though someone may have it right at the tip of his or her tongue. Often, a team will discuss an issue for far too long. They'll be stuck and no one will be offering solutions, when suddenly the quietest person in the room might speak up and suggest something. There might be a silence, then someone who says, "That's a good idea" and everyone agrees. Don't be afraid to take a shot. Yours might be the good idea.

One important point: When the issue is completely solved, someone must make the solution statement. For example, in the case of John being in the wrong seat, someone states the solution: "Barbara will sit down with John and discuss the warehouse seat issue, offer him the assistant manager seat, and see if he wants it. If not, we will part ways." You'll know after the statement that the problem is solved because you'll hear the sweet sound of agreement in the room. The issue is then owned by someone (in this case, Barbara), it's added to the To-Do List, and it gets done. Occasionally after the solution statement, someone will say, "Wait a minute, that is not what I heard," and the discussion will begin again. That's okay. You're creating clarity and getting everyone on the same page. Be patient.

The Issues Solving Track always follows the three steps: identify, discuss, and solve. The acronym for the track is IDS. As you move forward in mastering the Six Key Components, IDS will become an important aspect of your day-to-day running of the business. From now on, when faced with an issue, you simply "IDS it."

The power and simplicity of IDS is demonstrated by two EOS clients who do business together. They were facing some tough issues, so they scheduled a meeting. They sat down in the conference room, and one walked up to the whiteboard and wrote this:

$$I$$
$$D$$
$$S$$

The other smiled, and they went to work and resolved all of their issues. Not only does the Issues Solving Track work internally, but it works externally as well. The ability to "IDS it" became a common language between the two of them, and it's helped them not only to achieve resolution, but also to get there faster.

THE PERSONAL ISSUES SOLVING SESSION

Building a healthy team is not always a smooth process. If a team is not opening up, it might be because two individuals don't get along. They may even be at odds with one another. When this situation occurs, you must resolve the tension. Sometimes it's the only obstacle holding you back from being a functional, cohesive team. And you need a functional, cohesive team to be a healthy, growing company.

A personal issues solving session usually provides the remedy. This is an opportunity for the two people involved to come together to clear the air and resolve their differences. It's recommended that you have a third party facilitate the session.

1. Have each person prepare and then share with the other what he or she believes the other's three greatest strengths and three greatest weaknesses are.

2. List all the issues and solve them.

3. List the action items from the solutions.

4. Meet 30 days later to make certain that the action
   items have been accomplished.

Nine out of 10 times, their differences will be resolved. In rare cases, they can't be, and you have a tough decision to make because one must go for the greater good of the team. The analogy of the dying plant applies here. Once you cut off the dying limb, the plant flourishes, just as your team will. This is sometimes a hard pill to swallow, but, assuming you've conducted the personal issues solving session and exhausted every other option, it's what's best for the health of the team. Hopefully, the dismissed member can be relocated to another team in the organization.

Even in a healthy company, though, not everyone is going to get along like best friends. We are talking solely about building productive business relationships, as well as any personal issues severe enough to hinder the team from being frank about the company's needs.

With the Issues Component clear, you can create an open and honest organization that comfortably calls out issues and uses the Issues List and the Issues Solving Track to document and eliminate them. You're growing closer to reaching your full potential as a business.

You are now ready to work on the most neglected component of all, the secret ingredient of building a successful, well-run business: process.

SUMMARY

THE ISSUES COMPONENT

THE ISSUES LIST
- Open and honest
- Three types of Issues Lists

THE ISSUES SOLVING TRACK
- Identify
- Discuss
- Solve
- No tangents
- The 10 commandments of solving issues
- Personal issues solving session

CHAPTER 7

THE
PROCESS COMPONENT

FINDING YOUR *WAY*

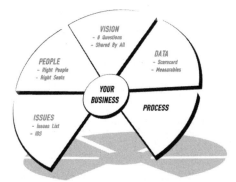

When Jim Weichert, the founder of Weichert, Realtors, one of the largest real estate companies in the world with over 19,000 salespeople and over 500 offices, was asked the secret of his success, he gave a one-word answer: consistency. That means consistency works. Consistency allows him to scale his business. As a result, he has built a solid organization that has endured for almost four decades.

Nothing can be fine-tuned until it's first consistent. The Process Component is strengthened through your understanding of the handful of core processes (on average, about seven) that make up your unique business model. You then have to make sure that everyone in your organization understands them, values them, and follows them. This component is the most neglected one, often taken for granted and undervalued by entrepreneurs and leaders. Yet the successful ones see what process can do for them. By not giving this component your full attention, it's costing you money, time, efficiency, and control.

Imagine once again that you could rise above and look down on your organization. How would it look? What are all of the moving parts? You should take this high-level view from time to time and appreciate what you have. Sometimes you can take what's been built for granted. To paraphrase philosopher and logician Kurt Gödel, you can't be in a system while at the same time understanding the system you're in. In other words, you need to raise your head from time to time and see the system for what it is, whether it's good or bad. We are normally so buried in the day-to-day scramble that we never take the time to do this. Yet, you'll see something new every time you do.

A typical organization operates through a handful of core processes. How these processes work together is its unique system. To break through the ceiling and build a well-oiled machine, you need to possess the ability to systemize. That is what this chapter is all about: helping you systemize what you've built. You'll discover different ways to improve upon your processes, simplify them, apply technology to them, and, most important of all, make them consistent throughout your organization.

Michael Gerber, author of *The E-Myth* and *The E-Myth Revisited*, calls this your franchise prototype. To the degree you can clarify your systems and hone them, you will run your business as opposed to having your business run you. The culmination of identifying, documenting, and having everyone follow the core processes of your business is your *Way*. When you have a clear *Way*, you immediately increase the value of your business, strengthen your control over it, and give yourself options. From there, you may grow the business, let someone else run it, sell it, or simply take more time off.

Countless business owners complain about their lack of control or freedom and yet, in the same breath, discount the value of process. It's like the story of the dog sitting on a nail. A gentleman walks up to a farmhouse. On the porch is an old man sitting in his rocking chair, and next to him is his old dog. The old dog is moaning, so the gentleman asks the old man why. "It's because he's sitting on a nail," the old man replies. "Why doesn't he move?" asks the gentleman. "Because it's not hurting enough for him to move."

Those business owners complaining about lack of control and freedom need to get off the nail and work on systemizing their businesses. In many organizations, people do their jobs however they want, resulting in tremendous inefficiencies and inconsistencies being embedded in the system. If they really saw all the variations, most business owners would be shocked. Many of them are just plain afraid to uncover what's really going on. They cross their fingers and hope that the company will keep chugging along.

A good example of a company that gained the power of the Process Component is Franklin Communities. It owns and manages eight manufactured-home communities. Despite being in a stereotyped business, owners Ron and Andy Blank have broken the mold. They run a tight ship. They implement every EOS tool to the letter. With the help of an amazing and tenacious operations person, Shelley Taylor, they created their Way and ran with it. With the help of a strong sales team led by Larry Lawson, each of the eight managers runs his or her communities by the book. The result is an occupancy rate that has the competition scratching their heads. While the industry's occupancies are dropping, Franklin's have steadily increased over the last four years.

To systemize your organization through your core processes, you must take two major steps. First, you have to document the core processes. Second, you have to ensure that they are followed by all. Let's start with documenting.

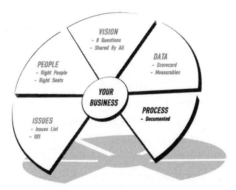

DOCUMENTING YOUR CORE PROCESSES
There are three stages in documenting your *Way*. First, identify your core processes. Then break down what happens in each one and document it. Finally, compile the information into a single package for everyone in your company.

IDENTIFY YOUR CORE PROCESSES
To start off, schedule an hour with your leadership team. This is not an assignment to delegate to one person. Take this initial step together so that you're calling your core processes the same thing. Entrepreneurs tend to claim

they already know what the processes are; I frequently get resistance on the need to call this meeting at all. Every time I suggest it, the reaction is, "Oh, we can do that in five minutes." I've yet to see a team do it in less than an hour.

Here's why. Your leadership team needs to identify and *agree* on what to call your core processes. Once you start the discussion, you're going to find you have different names for them and lack consensus on how many there are.

Your core processes typically include the following:

> **The HR process** is the way you search, find, hire, orient, manage, review, promote, retain, and fire people.

> **The marketing process** is the way you get your message to your target audience and generate interest in what you do and prospects for your salespeople.

> **The sales process** is the way you convert a prospect into a customer.

> **The operations processes** are the way you make your product or provide your service to your customer. There are typically one to three core processes within operations (e.g., project management, logistics, warehouse, distribution, service technicians, account management, service delivery, production, quality control, customer service).

> **The accounting process** is the flow and management of all monies coming in and going out.

> **The customer-retention process** is the proactive way that you take care of your customers after your product or service has been delivered and the way you retain customers so that they continue to come back and send you referrals.

No matter how many core processes you have, you need to identify the ones that address every activity going on in the business. Then list them in one document and make sure that your leadership team is 100 percent on the same page with the amount, the names, and what they are.

It's surprising how productive this step is. The exercise creates clarity of thought that is then put down in black and white. You will find it to be worth every minute of the hour you spend. You will realize a return on the time invested quickly as a result of everyone immediately speaking the same language.

Now that you've identified each core process and have a name for each one, everyone must call each of them by the exact same name from this day forward. If the way you manage your accounts is called the Customer Care Process, everyone must call it that. Just by calling your core processes by consistent names, you reduce complexity and increase efficiency in the organization.

DOCUMENT EACH OF THE CORE PROCESSES

In this step, the Accountability Chart comes into play. The person that is accountable for a certain process takes charge of documenting it. The head of sales and marketing takes the sales process and the marketing process. The head of operations takes the one to three operations processes, and so on. The integrator usually owns the entire project, making sure everyone is clear and on track.

To avoid wasting time, make sure you've completed the first step of identifying your core processes before you start documenting. A single example will show why. One client skipped Step 1 and went ahead and documented all the procedures in the organization. When the client was done, it had 100 separate procedures documented on its intranet. This work was not a total waste, but once the client went back to Step 1 and agreed on its seven core processes, each of the 100 procedures suddenly took on meaning because it became a part of one of their seven core processes. The client found that the procedures were much better organized, and could be transferred to all of its 120 employees. Still, it would have saved a lot of time and effort to identify the core processes first.

When documenting the processes, you should follow the 20/80 rule. That means document the 20 percent that produces 80 percent of the results. In other words, document at a very high level. You should not be creating a 500-page document. The 20/80 rule gives you the highest return on your time invested. The trap many organizations fall into is wasting valuable time trying to document 100 percent of everything. If you document 100 percent of a core process, it might take 30 pages. If you document the most important 20 percent, you should need around six pages.

A similar common problem is trying to document every single little detail down to the nth degree. This is overkill. You just need to capture the basic steps in the process, because the real problem is that people are skipping steps, and not always on purpose. Festering problems then blow up weeks or months down the road. In the heat of the uproar, you treat the symptom and not the root cause, which was that someone skipped a step. There is always an uncomfortable laugh when I share this truth. You need to document the steps in the process at a very high level, with several bullets under each step, which are procedures. This way, you can make sure everyone is following the process.

What you're illustrating are the basic guideposts to helping your people become consistent and efficient in your organization. The following is an example of a documented process:

THE HR PROCESS
Step 1: The Search
- Define role/job description/salary (the seat)
- Decide search medium
- Begin search
- E-mail 20 sphere/peers

Step 2: Interviewing
- Screen résumés
- Initial interview/profiling tools
- Second interview
- Check references
- CEO interview/core values speech

Step 3: Hiring
- Eight-hour on-the-job trial

- Decision
- 90-day trial

Step 4: Orientation
- HR policy/review employee manual
- Benefits review/forms
- Position training
- CEO orientation (company story/culture)

Step 5: Quarterly Reviews
- Manager fills out the People Analyzer in preparation for the review
- Follow the review checklist
- Review the People Analyzer
- Document the review and have it signed by all parties
- File review with HR department

Step 6: Termination
- Three-strike rule with documentation
- Terminate upon third strike
- Contact legal counsel
- Meet with employee/have HR present
- Exit interview
- Document termination and have it signed by all parties

Step 7: Ongoing Benefits Management
- 401K management
- Bonus plan
- Health insurance
- Employee files

In the end, each core process will run between two and 10 pages. Operations processes are usually the longest. Don't be totally constricted by the 20/80 rule. Include whatever you feel is necessary. Just make sure you keep it simple.

Once you start to document, you're going to uncover some hidden bones. Some steps will be in place that don't have to be. You won't understand how the heck they ever got there in the first place. When you ask why, you'll hear responses such as, "Well, we've always done it that way."

A man was once with his wife's family for Thanksgiving. During the preparation of the meal, he observed his wife cutting the back of a ham off before putting it in the oven. Curious, he asked her why she cut the back off the ham. She responded, "It's tradition. It's the way we've always done it in our family." Her mother had just arrived, so he took the opportunity to go over and ask why they cut off the back of a ham. She said, "It's tradition. It's the way we've always done it." Fortunately, his wife's grandmother was there as well, so he went to her and asked the same question. She replied, "Once upon a time, the pan was too small, and it was the only way to get the ham to fit in the pan."

Your people doing things because they've always done them that way is not good enough. With the opportunity to build a well-oiled machine, you must now be able to show them a better way.

As you simplify, most of the time you will find that your core processes are too complex. By documenting the process, you will find many opportunities to dumb them down by eliminating redundant steps, taking out any confusion and any complexity. The goal is to streamline.

Eliminate steps, condense steps, and put checklists in place where possible. Some steps in your processes will easily be converted to checklists that can be used on the floor or in the field. You should make your processes bulletproof so that no one can screw them up.

> Checklists have been an extremely effective tool for my clients to create consistency, quality control, and repeatable results. Please consider this heavily when documenting your core processes. There's a reason pilots and health care professionals use them. Countless studies have shown the considerable difference between using them or not. Use them for proposals, events, project management, and account management, to name a few.

Another advantage of simplifying each of the processes is to discover where technology can be applied. To connect core processes, or to enhance them on their own, realizes efficiencies and increases your profitability. There are great software systems that can connect your core processes and eliminate redundant steps, but make sure the investment of time and money will actually produce a return. Don't implement technology for technology's sake, leading to unnecessary headaches.

In my previous business, I made a move that I call the $45,000 Mistake. We needed a technology to manage The List that was created from our target market, as covered in Chapter 3. We kept a tremendous amount of information and history on our clients and prospects. We also needed to tie all of our North American trainers together.

I engaged an organization that claimed to have the latest and greatest technology. They were going to create the ideal software for us from scratch. This software would connect sales, marketing, and operations. After months and months of work and $45,000 spent creating the software, we scrapped it. Instead, we used a simple $500 off-the-shelf product that did everything we needed. The mistake I made was in not taking a close look at the process and the market for software. I got too caught up in the sizzle of what that particular software company was promising.

Technology must improve your *Way*. That means you must research and then decide based on creating efficiencies and simplification, not hype.

The other reason you must document and simplify your processes is that your business has to become self-sustaining. It has to be able to run without you. You have to get your key processes out of your head and onto paper. God forbid something happens to you or any of your people. If one of you disappeared tomorrow, could someone step in and pick up right where you left off? They should be able to, and by doing this step, you'll ensure that they can.

PACKAGE IT

Good news! Now that your core processes are documented, Step 3 is the easiest of all. Here's where you take all of the great work you've done in Steps 1 and

2 and package it. The titles of your core processes now become your table of contents. Each documented process in Step 2 becomes one of your sections. You put them in a binder or on your company intranet. On the cover, put your company name followed by the word "Way." If your company name is the ABC Company, then it should read "The ABC Company Way."

Your *Way* is now ready to use for reference and training. That's when the real magic happens. Now, everyone in the company can be trained to follow the correct process. This happened at an upscale pub and billiards restaurant called Roosevelt's. After co-owner Bill Gitre got his team in place, they went to work on documenting and simplifying their Way. The business model has become successful enough that they are now opening a second location.

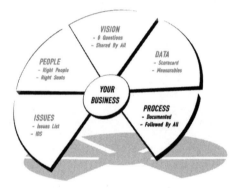

FOLLOWED BY ALL

When everyone follows their process, it's much easier for managers to manage, troubleshoot, identify and solve issues, and therefore grow the business. The clear lines of process enable you to let go and gain more control. Your business now becomes more scalable, which means that you can add more customers, transactions, revenue, and employees while reducing complexity.

In order to implement this crucial step, your leadership team must be convinced that everyone should follow one system. To convince your people to follow the process, your leadership team needs to be committed to managing all of the people to make the adjustment. If you are all committed, it will work. If you're not, it won't. "Do as I say, not as I do" is not effective management. I say this because most of the time this step fails because the owner or owners are not willing to follow the process.

Assuming you're convinced, the following step requires you to convince your people. You have to consider their point of view. If you didn't see the value in following a process before, how can you expect your people to see the value now? What you need to show is how the new system will create efficiencies to make their lives easier and the company more successful. They need to understand how the processes tie together into a complete system.

You shouldn't expect them to put you on their shoulders and carry you out of the room cheering, but do expect them to follow their assigned processes. While this isn't quite like announcing a company-wide 25 percent raise, you should present it with the same enthusiasm. If you have the right people in the right seats, they will see the value, appreciate it, and benefit from it.

One of the best ways to convince them is by creating a clear visual of what your *Way* looks like. Business processes are often intangible and therefore tough for people to understand. To the degree that you can illustrate what it looks like, you will accomplish this objective.

Sachse Construction came up with a great illustration. Owner Todd Sachse created a model of how all of the processes worked together in his organization. When he did his presentation on the importance of everyone following a process, his visual showed how every time a person follows a step in the process, it affects others. He called it the Circle of Life. Just as in nature, everyone in the organization depends on each other to thrive. By everyone following their process, everyone's life is ultimately going to be better. The opposite holds true as well. When someone doesn't follow the process, it has a negative effect on others in the organization. This knowledge actually motivates his people to work together and help make each process better. As a result, all processes in his Way are understood, embraced, and followed by everyone in his organization.

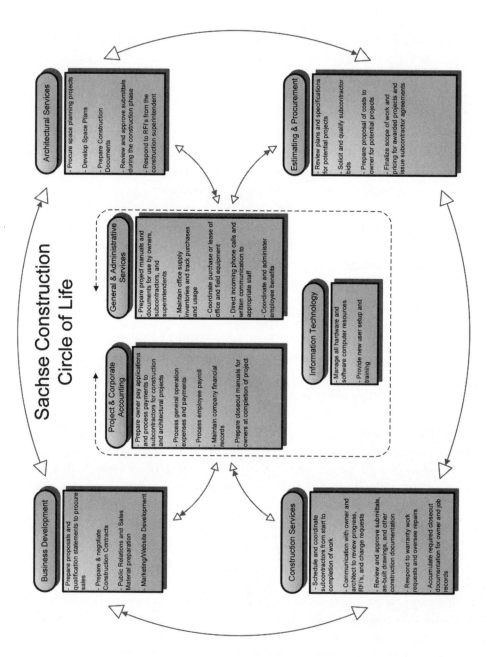

Sachse Construction
Circle of Life

Architectural Services
- Procure space planning projects
- Develop Space Plans
- Prepare Construction Documents
- Review and approve submittals during the construction phase
- Respond to RFI's from the construction superintendent

Estimating & Procurement
- Review plans and specifications for potential projects
- Solicit and qualify subcontractor bids
- Prepare proposal of costs to owner for potential projects
- Finalize scope of work and pricing for awarded projects and issue subcontractor agreements

General & Administrative Services
- Prepare project manuals and documents for use by owners, subcontractors, and superintendents
- Maintain office supply inventories and track purchases and usage
- Coordinate purchase or lease of office and field equipment
- Direct incoming phone calls and written communication to appropriate staff
- Coordinate and administer employee benefits

Information Technology
- Manage all hardware and software computer resources
- Provide new user setup and training

Project & Corporate Accounting
- Prepare owner pay applications and process payments to subcontractors for construction and architectural projects
- Process general operation expenses and payments
- Process employee payroll
- Maintain company financial records
- Prepare closeout manuals for owners at completion of project

Business Development
- Prepare proposals and qualification statements to procure sales
- Prepare & negotiate Construction Contracts
- Public Relations and Sales Material preparation
- Marketing/Website Development

Construction Services
- Schedule and coordinate subcontractors from start to completion of work
- Communication with owner and architect to review progress, RFI's, and change requests
- Review and approve submittals, as-built drawings, and other construction documentation
- Respond to warranty work requests and oversee repairs
- Accumulate required closeout documentation for owner and job records

"FOLLOWED BY ALL" ACTION STEPS

1. Create your Circle of Life visual.

2. Schedule a company meeting to share your *Way* or share it at your next quarterly company meeting.

3. Retrain everyone.

4. Manage your people to follow the processes.

With your business systemized, you can better troubleshoot when problems arise, since many of them result from process-related issues. For instance, maybe there's an invoice that didn't go out due to the customer service representative not forwarding a copy of the order form to accounting. Track the problem to the source and solve it. When a problem occurs, you can go right to the step that is not working and alter or eliminate it. In some cases, you may add a new step. But you're simply performing maintenance at this point. You now have everything you need to get your *Way* followed by all.

Strengthening the Process Component will give you more control. You will have options with your business: to grow it, step away from it, sell it, maintain it, franchise it, or duplicate it in another city. Whichever option you choose, your organization's value has increased. Your organization will be worth more as a result. This is what people that purchase businesses are looking for: a turnkey system. For instance, the owners of Image One were approached by a billion-dollar publicly traded company in the same industry and eventually sold to them. The president of the division at the time, who previously worked for Jack Welch at GE, said that Image One was one of the best-run companies he'd ever seen.

With the mastery of the Process Component, you're closing in on achieving your destination.

You're now ready to bring it all down to the ground with the final piece of the puzzle—the Traction Component.

SUMMARY

THE PROCESS COMPONENT

DOCUMENTING YOUR CORE PROCESSES
- Identify your core processes
- Document and simplify them (20/80 rule)
- Package them into one source

FOLLOWED BY ALL
- Create your "Circle of Life" model
- Train everyone
- Manage people to follow the core processes

CHAPTER 8

THE
TRACTION COMPONENT

FROM LUFTMENSCH
TO ACTION!

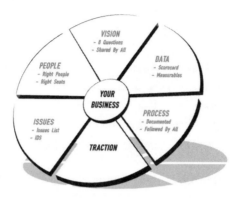

ction is the process of doing. That's what this chapter is all about.
Gaining traction means making your vision a reality. At this moment,
your vision is crystal clear, you have the right people in the right
seats, you're managing data, you're solving your issues, and you've defined
your *Way* of doing business and everyone is following it. Now you're ready
to master organizational traction, the final piece of the puzzle. Mastering the
first five components was essential before tackling this component, because
without them, you might gain traction, but in the wrong direction. When
the first five components are strong, you will take off in the right direction—
toward your vision.

The ability to create accountability and discipline, and then execute, is the area
of greatest weakness in most organizations. If I asked you to rate the level of
accountability in your organization on a scale of 1 to 10, with 10 being your
perfect level of accountability, how would you rate it? Successful leaders rate
themselves high because they know how to gain traction. When meeting with
the average new client for the first time, though, they typically rate their current
accountability at 4.

This is a real shame, because the world is filled with many great visions.
Unfortunately, most will go unrealized due to an inability to gain traction.
Visionaries like to stay on a high plane, not at ground level. After more than 20
years of observing failures, I realized how to bridge the gap between vision and
execution.

I recently learned a word that makes the point. Luftmensch is a Yiddish word made from two others; *luft* means "air" and mensch means "person." A *luftmensch* is an "air-person," someone who has his or her head in the clouds. I don't mean this as an insult. Ideas come from having your head in the clouds. Most visionaries would agree with me. That is their gift, their strength, and their value. Nothing exists without visionaries. Yet once the vision is clear, you need to go from *luftmensch* to action.

Most leaders know that bringing discipline and accountability to the organization will make people a little uncomfortable. That's an inevitable part of creating traction. What usually holds an organization back is the fear of creating this discomfort. But you don't have any other option if you want to build a great company. If you can accept the fact that you're going to make people a little uncomfortable for a short time, the solution is actually straightforward. You need to implement two simple practices.

As with all the steps along the way, this one requires a total commitment from the leadership team. There will be far too many opportunities to pull back and retreat. If your leadership can stay the course, however, within months your people will appreciate the increased accountability, improved communication, and solid results. The discomfort you were concerned about turns out to be not nearly as bad as you thought. And truth be told, the people who continue to resist are either the wrong people or in the wrong seat.

This is one of the secrets to the EOS methodology: We don't let leadership teams turn back. For that, they eventually thank us and say they don't know how they could previously have lived without this high level of traction, accountability, and results.

What are the two disciplines needed to gain traction? First, everyone must set specific, measurable priorities. Second, you must meet better as an organization. These two essentials are called: Rocks and a Meeting Pulse.

Before we dig deeper into each of the disciplines, I offer some before-and-after statements from clients that have fully implemented these traction tools. You or your people may relate to them.

BEFORE TRACTION

No Accountability

- "I really didn't know who I was accountable to."

- "Although we agreed to meet on a regular basis, in actuality we didn't. We lacked accountability and focus."

- "Before Rocks, there was no clarity."

Poor Communication

- "I felt alone in my understanding of what was needed in the company. I also was misunderstood."

- "I've worked here for over 20 years, and before Rocks, I was never in the loop."

Stagnation

- "We were fairly disciplined about creating one-year goals, but would frequently find ourselves at the end of the year having made no substantive progress toward those goals. It was tough to stay focused on them throughout the year."

- "We had no clear direction or priority. Everything was important, and as a result our efforts were not directed where they were most effective. 'We suffered from the classic 'show up and work for work's sake.'"

- "*Everything* was a priority."

Chaos

- "It was tough to get out of the day-to-day emergencies and focus on the most important priorities."

- "We didn't meet very often. Coming to a decision could take weeks, and we always had to re-present the information."

- "Things slipped through the cracks."

- "No structure, lack of communication around goals and issues. Problems were not resolved, and they just stacked up. We had no method to measure results."

- "We were very reactionary, dealing with the problem of the week or month."

- "It was not clear whose job was whose, so I always felt everything was on my shoulders and I had to do it all."

AFTER TRACTION
Accountability
- "After Rocks, everyone on the team has responsibility, clarity, and timing on what has to get done. Also, each team member is clear on his or her accountability. Everyone is on the same page."

- "I see us now working more as a cohesive unit with purpose and direction. We are working toward closure with issues, employee accountability, and job responsibilities. We now have some organization with a focus on what we do best."

- "With the Rocks and Meeting Pulse in place, I feel the ability for me and my team to focus better on the big-picture items. More is getting done in the same amount of time, and we have a heightened sense of urgency to get things done by certain due dates."

Communication
- "The meetings are 90 minutes and no longer. It's taking time, but I can now see the benefits of having weekly meetings as opposed to monthly."

- "Now at least with the Rocks and weekly meetings, I get a sense of priority, and I know what direction the company is going."

- "The Meeting Pulses have really served as an excellent communication vehicle to cascade messages within our rapidly changing environment."

Organization

- "Rocks gave me a way to check in with my reports and drive better results in a highly consistent manner."

- "Life after Rocks is very rewarding! All players are on the same page. We are focused toward a common goal. There is clarity in both expectations and direction. We can clearly identify weak performers and those that do not fit within our organization. Truly, it is like night and day!"

- "Rocks keep everyone focused, and allow us to work toward one-year goals in bite-sized chunks. Rocks have become the measurable and the lingo of our organization. We see employees seriously approaching their Rocks with a sense of pride and commitment."

Traction

- "Now I feel that the forward momentum is turbocharging our organization by getting everyone to help row the boat."

- "With Rocks, we have found the way to achieve goals, hold people accountable, and move in a positive direction on a continuous basis."

- "Now we are getting ahead of the problems and pushing into prediction and working on our systems. We have more time to work forward, not deal with past problems."

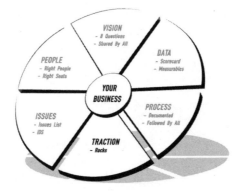

ROCKS

With a clear long-term vision in place, you're ready to establish short-term priorities that contribute to achieving your vision. You will establish the three to seven most important priorities for the company, the ones that must be done in the next 90 days. Those priorities are called Rocks.

One of our students at the sales training company illustrated the power of setting 90-day priorities. In the days when his family picked cotton by hand, the student said he would stand at the foot of the field, look out at the acres and acres of cotton, and feel overwhelmed by the work that needed to be done.

To make the prospect of picking all those acres less overwhelming, someone would pick up a stick and throw it as far as he or she could. Then everybody would just put their heads down and "pick to the stick." When they got there, they'd pick up that stick, throw it out again, and repeat the process.

That's why you create a 90-Day World. Rather than be overwhelmed by the monumental task of accomplishing your vision, this allows you to break it down into bite-size chunks called Rocks and focus on making it to the stick.

Your company will have Rocks, each member of your leadership team will have Rocks, and your employees will also have Rocks. The reason to limit Rocks to three to seven (preferably closer to three) is that you're going to break the organization of the habit of trying to focus on everything at once. It simply can't be done. By limiting priorities, you can focus on what is most important. With the increased intensity of focusing on a limited number of Rocks, your people will accomplish more. Remember the old saying: When everything is important, nothing is important. The way you move the company forward is one 90-day period at a time.

Rocks create a short-term focus similar to the point I raised earlier from Al Ries's book *Focus*. To the degree that you focus everyone in one direction, you'll gain the power of that laser beam, gaining traction toward your goals.

Once your vision is clear, you will set better Rocks. Setting these priorities becomes simple. Once you set the company Rocks and then the leadership team's Rocks, you then communicate these Rocks to the entire organization so they can set theirs. This process creates alignment. The exact process for establishing Rocks as a team and then rolling out this process organization-wide will be explained in this chapter.

By the way, it doesn't matter what you call these priorities; however, most companies really like calling them Rocks. I learned the term from Verne Harnish, the author of *Mastering the Rockefeller Habits*. Verne got it from an analogy in Stephen Covey's book *First Things First*. Picture a glass cylinder set on a table. Next to the cylinder are rocks, gravel, sand, and a glass of water. Imagine the glass cylinder as all of the time you have in a day. The rocks are your main priorities, the gravel represents your day-to-day responsibilities, the sand represents interruptions, and the water is everything else that you get hit with during your workday. If you, as most people do, pour the water in first, the sand in second, the gravel in third, and the rocks last, what happens? Those big priorities won't fit inside the glass cylinder. That's your typical day.

What happens if you do the reverse? Work on the big stuff first: Put the rocks in. Next come the day-to-day responsibilities: Add the gravel. Now dump in the sand, all those interruptions. Finally, pour the water in. Everything fits in the glass cylinder perfectly; everything fits in your day perfectly. The bottom line is that you need to work on the biggest priorities—your Rocks—first. Everything else will fall into place.

Less is always better, and a few priorities are better than many. Do less, accomplish more. Most organizations start out the year with a huge ball of priorities and get very little done by the end of the year. By coming up with Rocks every quarter, you create a 90-Day World.

The process works like this: Your team meets for a full day every 90 days. You review your vision, and then determine what the Rocks are for the organization for the next 90-day period to keep you on track for your vision.

ESTABLISHING YOUR ROCKS
STEP 1
After reviewing your V/TO and getting on the same page, your leadership team lists everything on the whiteboard that has to be accomplished in the next 90

days. On average, you'll discover about 10 to 20 things that you'd like to close out, although one client came up with 75.

STEP 2
With that list of 10 to 20 items in front of you, discuss, debate, and determine the most important priorities for the company in the next 90 days. Make a decision on each one whether to keep it, kill it, or combine it as a company Rock for the quarter. You make as many passes at the list as necessary until you're down to three to seven. As a result, the right ones will rise to the top.

STEP 3
Once you've narrowed your list, set the date that the Rocks are due. This is typically by the end of the quarter (i.e., March 31, June 30, September 30, and December 31). Now define each one by making sure the objectives are clear. This is vital.

A Rock is specific, measurable, and attainable. For example: "Close three core accounts" or "Hire a new controller." A Rock is not a to-do that is open-ended or vague. "Start working on the Customer Service Process" is not specific, measurable, and attainable, and is therefore not a good Rock.

A Rock must be clear so that at the end of the quarter, there is no ambiguity whether it was done or not. Here is an example of four company Rocks that were set and defined:

Company Rocks due by March 31
  1. Close $1 million in new business
  2. Document delivery process and train all
  3. Narrow CFO candidates to two
  4. Implement new information systems software

STEP 4
Assign who owns each Rock. This is vital for clear accountability. Each of the three to seven company Rocks must be owned by one and only one person on the leadership team. When more than one person is accountable for a Rock, no

one is accountable. The owner is the person who drives the Rock to completion during the quarter by putting together a timeline, calling meetings, and pushing people. At the end of the quarter, the owner is the one that everyone looks at to assure the Rock was completed.

STEP 5

Once the company Rocks are set, the members of the leadership team each set their own Rocks. They first carry forward any company Rocks that they own to their individual list of Rocks and then come up with their most important three to seven. Some of the Rocks that were discarded in Step 2 for the company can end up becoming individual Rocks for leadership team members. Please remember—no more than three to seven. Any Rock candidates left over on the original list that did not get picked up can be carried forward to the next quarter by putting them on the V/TO Issues List.

STEP 6

When all that great work is done, you then create what is called the Rock Sheet, which is just a landscaped piece of paper. At the top are the organization's Rocks, and below that are each of the leadership team's individuals Rocks. This Rock Sheet is brought into your weekly meetings to review your Rocks. It will help create clear accountability and focus on what is the highest priority in the organization. With that, a wall goes up, and no one is allowed to throw anything else over it, whether it's a genius-level new idea or a hand grenade. Once the priorities are set for this quarter, *no new priorities can be added*! If someone does try to throw something else over, you get to throw it back because you all agreed on the current Rocks as being the most important priorities for this quarter. New ideas and thoughts that arise during the quarter should be put on the V/TO Issues List for next quarter. This approach will help you create laser focus for your organization. The following is an example of an effective Rock Sheet.

Rocks due by March 31, 2007

Company Rocks	Owner
1. Close $1 million in new business	BL
2. Document delivery process and train all	AM
3. Narrow CFO candidates to two	JK
4. Implement new IS software	SP

Bill's Rocks

1. Close $1 million in new business
2. 10 new prospects in the pipeline
3. Hire one new salesperson

John's Rocks

1. Narrow CFO candidates to two
2. Finalize and implement new hire orientation
3. Increase line of credit to $1 million

Amy's Rocks

1. Document delivery process and train all
2. Create customer feedback system
3. Update database
4. Proactively contact top 10 clients
5. Revise and recommunicate Accountability Chart

Sam's Rocks

1. Implement new IS software
2. Roll out our new website
3. Retrain all on A/R and A/P policy
4. Finalize new client contracts

STEP 7

Share the company Rocks with the entire organization. As you learned in the Vision Component, the vision must be shared by all. Every quarter you should meet with the entire organization for your state-of-the-company meeting for no more than 45 minutes to share successes, progress, and the V/TO and to unveil the company Rocks for the quarter. Remember, people sometimes have to hear something seven times before they really hear it for the first time, and this is one of the ways they will ultimately share the vision.

STEP 8

Have each department set their Rocks as a team. Just as the leadership team sets their Rocks, each department team follows the exact same process to set theirs as well. In the end, each employee will have his or her own Rocks for the quarter. Please note that while the company and leadership team members should have three to seven Rocks, everyone else in the company should have one to three.

ROCK TRAPS AND PITFALLS

Your organization needs to avoid certain problems when establishing and carrying out its Rocks.

- **Garbage in, garbage out.** For every tool in the Entrepreneurial Operating System (EOS), you will get out what you put in. If you set the wrong Rocks, you will spend an entire quarter pointed in the wrong direction. Make sure you spend the necessary time setting the right ones. Do not rush the process.

- **It takes two quarters to master Rocks.** You will not master the process the first time around. Be patient, because true mastery comes from experience. You need to learn from two quarters with only your leadership team setting Rocks before you roll out the Rocks process to everyone else. You will make some mistakes and it's important you learn from those mistakes first so that you can be a better teacher for your people.

- **Commitment fizzle.** Make sure that when rolling out Rocks, you're fully committed to them every quarter. Some clients start off with a bang and then don't commit to their quarterly routine. As a result they stop sharing them with everyone, and your people will end up feeling like the Rocks process was just another flavor-of-the-month idea.

- **Too many Rocks.** Don't give people outside of the leadership team more than three Rocks. The responsibility is too overwhelming for most employees to handle, and you would be violating the golden rule that less is more.

Image One's Rob Dube explains the cumulative power of all those Rocks: "One year during our annual all-company meeting, I had an idea to go around the room and ask every team member to tell us a few of the Rocks they accomplished during the year. While each person was talking, I was writing the Rock on the whiteboard. By the end, I was off the whiteboard and onto many pieces of paper from the flip chart! When you have a team of 35 people like we do, take that number and multiply it by two Rocks per person for a quarter, you get 70. Then multiply that by the number of quarters in a year, and you get 280! That is the magic number—we took 280 steps in the right direction over the past 12 months. Amazing!"

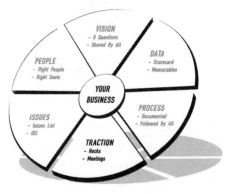

MEETING PULSE

For now and forever, let's dispel the myth that all meetings are bad, that meetings are a waste of time, and that there are already too many of them. The fact is that well-run meetings are the moment of truth for accountability. To gain traction, you'll probably need to meet even more than you presently do.

In Patrick Lencioni's book *Death by Meeting*, he opens the book by making a humorous observation. After hearing many leaders complain about meetings and saying things like, "If I didn't have to go to meetings, I'd like my job a lot more," Lencioni asks us to imagine hearing a surgeon saying to a nurse before surgery, "If I didn't have to operate on people, I might actually like this job." He then asks us to consider the fact that, for those of us who lead and manage organizations, meetings are pretty much what we do.

It's possible to hold extremely productive meetings that actually save time. In this chapter, you will combine the 90-Day World with a powerful tool, the Level 10 Meeting. Together, these will enable you to have great meetings that increase communication, accountability, team health, and results. As a result of meeting more and following the Meeting Pulse, everyone will get more done. The time you spend meeting will actually free up time for moving forward.

The Meeting Pulse is your organization's heartbeat. Rather than long, meandering meetings, a Meeting Pulse with a specific agenda throughout your departments will keep your organization healthy. A Meeting Pulse operates just like an EKG illustrating a spike. When people have to get something done for a meeting, they wait until the last minute and usually finish it—that's the spike. The more you can increase the meeting interval, the more spikes you get, and then the more business you'll finish. At first you'll resist these regular meetings, but as soon as they become a habit, you'll embrace them. You won't know how you could have lived without them in the past. I have seen this happen with every client. It's where the real magic happens.

The Meeting Pulse consists of two types of meetings. The first is quarterly and the second is weekly. Let's take them one at a time, starting with the quarterly.

THE 90-DAY WORLD

As a part of your vision, you created a three-year picture. After that came a one-year plan and now a 90-Day World, as illustrated by the model on the following page. The 90-day idea stems from a natural phenomenon—that human beings stumble, get off track, and lose focus roughly every 90 days. To address this aspect of human nature, you must implement a routine throughout the entire organization that creates a 90-Day World.

I first discovered its effectiveness in my own organization. After my first full-day meeting with my leadership team, we all came out laser-focused on where we were going as an organization and what we had to do. Roles and responsibilities were agreed upon. We were on the same page and fired up. But 90 days later, for some reason, we'd all started to wander off track. I couldn't explain why, so we held another meeting for a full day, pulling us all back together. We had a passionate, intense, productive meeting and got back on track again. Yet after another 90 days, I had to hold another meeting because I did not even recognize my team. "What happened to the people who were participating in that intense meeting 90 days ago?" I wondered. We couldn't be further off the same page. But just like clockwork, by the end of the meeting, we were fired up and on the same page yet again.

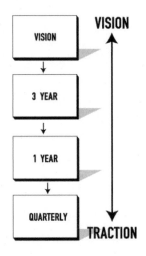

I soon realized it was a normal cycle. When I really thought about the problem, I noticed it affected my Entrepreneurs' Organization forum group, my friends, and my family. It seems to be human nature. Of the 1300 full-day sessions I've conducted, at least 900 have been quarterly sessions. People whose focus was clear in the prior quarterly session became unfocused by the following one. I would see absolute agreement on core issues the previous quarter and then total disagreement in the current one. By the end of the session, though, everyone would be back on track. In some situations, people didn't even remember agreeing. Fortunately, I kept very good notes and could prove that they did.

Realizing this cycle was normal, I changed my attitude. First, I stopped getting frustrated and accepted it. Second, I decided to put together a great agenda for a powerful quarterly meeting every time. Now all EOS clients follow this exact same agenda in their quarterlies.

One last point: If you don't continue to align quarterly, your organization will fragment to the point that you will get far off track, you will start to lose great people, you will lose sight of your vision, and you will end up right back where you started—in chaos.

To repeat, 90 days is about as long as a human being can stay focused. It's human nature, so stop fighting it and solve the problem by following the Quarterly Meeting Pulse, thereby creating a 90-Day World for your company.

In addition, I strongly recommend that you hold your quarterly meetings off-site. When you're at the office, there will be too many distractions to pull you back into the business. Being away provides a great opportunity for the team to truly work *on* the business.

THE EOS QUARTERLY MEETING PULSE

Who: The leadership team

Where: Off-site

Duration: Eight hours

Frequency: Every 90 days

Prework: Vision/Traction Organizer complete
(Everyone brings his or her issues and proposed priorities for the coming quarter)

THE QUARTERLY MEETING AGENDA
- Segue
- Review previous quarter
- Review the V/TO
- Establish next quarter's Rocks
- Tackle key issues
- Next steps
- Conclude

Segue

This is the transition from a full 90 days of working hard in the business to starting to work on the business. Each person should share three things: (1) best business and personal news in the last 90 days, (2) what is working and not working in the organization, and (3) expectations for the day. Not only will this elevate everyone to working *on* the business, but it will also help set the stage for the quarterly meeting.

One person might say during his or her segue, "The best business news is that we landed the ABC account. What I feel is working is the new customer relationship management software. What I feel is not working are our delivery times, the customer service department, and our inventory system. My expectation is to solve these three things once and for all. Plus, I'd like us to be a healthier leadership team." This, along with everyone's segue, sets the tone for the meeting.

Review Previous Quarter

Review all of your numbers (quarterly revenue, profit, gross margin, and any other relevant key numbers) and your Rocks (company and leadership teams on the Rock Sheet) from the previous quarter to confirm which ones were achieved and which were not. I highly recommend simply stating "done" or "not done" for each. This will give you a clear, black-and-white picture of how you performed. Don't get caught up in believing you can complete 100 percent of your Rocks every quarter. It's perfectionist thinking and not realistic. You always want to strive for 80 percent completion or better—that's enough to be truly great.

If you didn't complete 80% you need to understand why and learn from it. Look at the Rocks you didn't accomplish. Discuss why they weren't completed. The two most common reasons for not achieving a Rock are:

- *You took too much on and overshot*, which was poor prediction on your part. In this case, your team will need to become better at setting more realistic Rocks. The first time most clients set their Rocks, they almost always set them too high.

- *Someone dropped the ball.* In other words, the Rock was attainable, but the person in charge did not give it his or her all. In this case, you have an accountability issue, and you need to put it on the Issues List and solve it. In the long run, you will reach a point where every member of the leadership team always gives his or her maximum effort when owning a Rock.

You have one of three options with incomplete Rocks:

1. Carry the Rock forward to the next quarter.

2. If the Rock is 95 percent complete, completing the last 5 percent simply becomes an action item for the To-Do List.

3. Reassign the Rock to someone else.

Review the V/TO

The sole intent of reviewing the V/TO every quarter is to refresh your memory on the vision and to make sure that everyone is still on the same page. Within that framework, you will set much better Rocks for the next quarter. When people are not on the same page, discuss and debate until they are.

> Taking the necessary time to review the V/TO and get back on the same page in the quarterly meeting also leads to much better issue solving later in the session due to everyone having absolute clarity on the company's greater good.

In an open and honest environment, everyone must voice their opinions if they don't understand, don't agree, or have a concern with any item in the V/TO. If there is any confusion, you must solve the issue at that moment until everyone is in concert. A good V/TO review takes between 30 minutes and two hours, depending how much discussion is needed. Make certain you conclude the V/TO review by updating the eighth section, the Issues List. Remove any issues that have been solved and add any new ones. This will build your Issues List for the day.

Establish Next Quarter's Rocks

With the stage set from your segue, clarity on your results from the review of last quarter's Rocks, your vision clearly in mind after your review of the V/TO, and your Issues List in front of you, you now follow the Rock-setting process covered earlier in this chapter.

List everything that must get done this quarter. Decide to keep, kill, or combine everything on the list, boiling them down to the right three to seven Rocks for the company and assign ownership. From there, establish each leadership team member's Rocks and give them to one member to create the Rock Sheet.

Tackle Key Issues

With your Rocks set, you will have anywhere from one to four hours left in your meeting, depending on how long your V/TO review and Rock-setting took. It's now time to tackle all of your relevant issues for the quarter. What makes for great meetings is solving issues. Start by making sure that all of the issues are on the list. Ask the team for any issues they have on their minds if they haven't shared them already during the first half of the meeting.

You now go to the Issues List you have compiled, which includes issues from the first half of the meeting and all carryover issues from previous meetings that were listed on the V/TO Issues List. Remove all issues that were resolved by the creation of new Rocks.

Tackle the remaining issues following the Issues Solving Track—Identify, Discuss, and Solve (IDS). Establish the top three issues, then start with number one and work through the list in order of priority. For each issue, identify the real problem, then openly discuss all aspects of it, getting all opinions out on the table with no tangents. From there, move to solve the issue and make it go away forever. You will get through anywhere from one to 15 issues depending on the time you have and the magnitude of the issues.

Any issues you do not solve can simply be carried forward to your weekly Issues List or the V/TO Issues List, depending on their priority level. You will rarely solve them all. The important thing is to make sure you're solving them in order of priority.

Next Steps

This part of the quarterly meeting is typically short. Everyone discusses any next steps—who is doing what, and whether there are any messages to communicate to the organization based on the decisions made in the meeting.

For instance, if you solved the issue mentioned in the segue regarding the customer service department, in Next Steps you might confirm that the director of operations is going to meet with everyone in customer service and together strategize and implement a plan this quarter to create a world-class customer service department.

Conclude

In concluding the meeting, everyone shares three things: (1) feedback on the meeting, (2) whether their expectations were met or not, and (3) their rating on the meeting from 1 to 10. You want the standard to average above 8.

It's powerful how much the Quarterly Meeting Pulse can do for you. It focuses everyone on which direction you should row. You come out fired up and ready to take on the next quarter.

However, like clockwork, you're going to start getting off track again 90 days later. Some quarters, you may think that you don't need to meet. I can remember several times needing to convince my partners after they asked, "Why are we meeting again? Aren't things going pretty well?" Don't fall into this trap. You have to combat the human tendency to want to coast for a while and take a little pressure off. I have clients that call once in a while prior to a quarterly, saying they don't think they need to meet. After I convince them they do, in every case they have reported they were glad they did. I can't tell you how many times I've heard the words "Wow, and I didn't think we'd have anything to talk about this quarter!" at the end of a client quarterly session.

You're going to repeat that same Quarterly Meeting Pulse forever. You will find that the meetings keep getting better. With that routine in place, at the end of every year you will piggyback an extra day on the front end of your quarterly meeting for your annual planning. Annual Planning is an opportunity to build team health, reset the vision, and create a clear plan for the next year.

THE EOS ANNUAL MEETING PULSE

Who: The leadership team

Where: Off-site

Duration: Two days

Frequency: Every year

Prework: Bring completed Vision/Traction Organizer, proposed budget for next year, and thoughts on goals for next year.

THE ANNUAL PLANNING AGENDA: DAY ONE

- Segue
- Review previous year
- Team health building
- SWOT/Issues List
- V/TO (through one-year plan)

Segue

Each member of the leadership team shares three things: (1) the organization's three greatest accomplishments in the previous year, (2) his or her one greatest personal accomplishment for the year, and (3) his or her expectations for the two-day annual planning session.

The power of the annual segue, in addition to setting the stage and transitioning from working in the business to on the business, is that leaders have a chance to stop for a few minutes and reflect on the company's successes and progress over the previous year. After the segue, one client said, "I was actually feeling like we had a bad year until I listened to everyone share the business accomplishments. We actually had a pretty good year." This is typically the mindset after the segue, and that sets the tone for what follows.

Review Previous Year

Review the previous year's goals, the previous year's numbers (previous year's revenue, profit, gross margin, and other relevant key numbers), and last quarter's Rocks. You should be achieving 80 percent or better of your goals to truly be great. One of the ways you and your team will become better predictors of future events is by reviewing your results and addressing what worked and what didn't.

When you review your goals for the year, you must take the same approach as the Rock review. You want only black-or-white "done" or "not done" answers. This is one reason your goals must be very specific. If one of the goals for the year was "create a sales-focused organization," how can you determine if that was done or not? If the sales goal was "$2 million in new sales from the sales team and $300,000 from account managers," you can definitely determine if that was done.

Keep in mind your goals were set a year ago. Most people's memories aren't good enough to remember what the intention was that far back. You don't have to remember intentions if you have specific and measurable goals.

There's another reason to prefer specificity. You're trying to assess how you did in order to determine exactly your degree of success or failure so that you can get better at it next time. When the results are vague and debatable, it's far too difficult to see clearly what worked and what didn't. You then rationalize your way into believing the year was better than it was. When you have no real way to pinpoint what to improve upon, you aren't going to get better. So even if your first attempts to establish goals prove to be off the mark—sometimes way off the mark—keep trying. With practice, you'll learn to set targets that are truly specific, measurable, and attainable, which will make you great predictors and ultimately lead to a solid, well-run, and enduring organization.

Team Health Building

Many great team-building exercises are available. You may already have one. If you don't, I highly recommend an exercise I call One Thing. Each member of the team receives feedback from the others on his or her single greatest strength or most admirable ability and his or her biggest weakness or hindrance to the success of the company. The exercise is done out in the open, with the entire leadership team present. I believe the peer-evaluation methods that are conducted anonymously actually do more harm than good. This exercise has been done countless times with teams, and it always has produced great long-term results. Some clients have performed this exercise four years running at their Annual Planning Session, and the results get better every time.

After everyone has received the feedback from their team members, each then must choose one thing he or she will commit to doing differently in the coming year based on the feedback. It's short, simple, very powerful, and effective, and it leads to great insights with improved openness and honesty on the team. This exercise should take no longer than two hours.

> A great discipline I've used with my clients to assure full delivery to their commitments is to do a quick feedback exercise in each quarterly session. Each person states their commitment, and every member gives one-word feedback on how they are doing honoring it. They state either "better," "worse," or "same." It's a nice tap on the shoulder, and it substantially improves follow-through.

SWOT/Issues List

Provide an opportunity for everyone to share what they believe the organization's *strengths, weaknesses, opportunities,* and *threats* are. This is the classic SWOT analysis, a management tool for helping an organization take a good look at itself and clarify its current state, both good and bad. The most productive outcome of the SWOT analysis is the Issues List. Once you have listed everyone's opinions of the organization's strengths, weaknesses, opportunities, and threats, you extract all of the relevant issues for the coming year and create an Issues List for the Two-Day Planning Session. This list, along with all additional issues added throughout the session, should be added to your Issues List for the next day's Issues Solving.

V/TO (Through One-Year Plan)

At this point in the session, you challenge the company vision. This is the Annual Meeting Pulse, and nothing is sacred. Working your way through the V/TO, take a hard look at your core values, challenge the core focus, make sure everyone is still on board for the 10-year target, and confirm that the marketing strategy is still unique and valuable to the customer. Where you're not on the same page, discuss and debate until everyone is in sync.

Assuming you're all in agreement, you throw out the old Three-Year Picture and create a brand-new one. You want to make sure that everyone agrees on the same image three years from now. Once everyone's mind's eye can see it, the odds are greater that you will achieve it.

Once the new Three-Year Picture is clear, go to work on next year's plan. Set the revenue, profit, and numbers for the coming year and then set your three to seven most important goals. Remember, less is more, so be careful. One-year planning rarely takes more than two hours. Don't overthink it. When the vision is clear, the numbers and goals are right in front of you. You just have to put them down on paper and agree with them. In addition, make sure a budget exists to support the plan and that everyone is clear on their roles and responsibilities in the coming year. Let the Accountability Chart be your guide.

> Some clients wrestle with the approach of throwing out the old three-year picture and starting with a new one. It's important to take this approach for two reasons. One is that a full year has gone by and things have changed, so it's important to take all of your knowledge and experience and incorporate it into a newly created vision. The second reason is that you're smarter, better, faster planners than you were a year ago, and as a result, you'll do much better work.
>
> If it's important to you to hang onto the old three-year picture, I'd recommend that you cut and paste it into a document to hang onto personally and see how you did, but the above approach is what is recommended and most effective.

THE ANNUAL PLANNING AGENDA: DAY TWO

- Establish next quarter's Rocks
- Tackle key issues
- Next steps
- Conclude

Refer to the Quarterly Planning Agenda for details on the above agenda items.

Annual Planning Tips

- **Many times, the one-year planning portion of the V/TO carries over into Day Two.** Let it happen. You should not rush the process. You will have time on Day Two to complete the agenda if necessary.

- **Have dinner together as a team at the end of Day One.** Seize the opportunity to blow off steam after a day of intense thinking as well as to continue to build team health.

- **Get away for annual planning.** You don't necessarily have to travel across the country, but a hotel an hour or two away will lead to a more productive meeting. When you're removed from the office, you'll be able to turn the real world off for a full two days.

THE BUILDUP

By religiously implementing the Quarterly and Annual Meeting Pulse, you create a 90-Day World that will reap tremendous benefits for your organization. There is a hidden benefit as well, one that I don't even share with my clients. One of the main reasons that the Quarterly Meeting Pulse is so effective is what I call the buildup. With the prospect of a full day scheduled for the leadership team to meet, people prepare better for it without even knowing they are doing it. Their energy, fears, thoughts, issues, ideas, and excitement all start to build toward this special event. As a result, the meeting is much more effective.

The opposite also holds true. That is, if you don't tell anyone you are having a quarterly meeting and simply call them into a full-day meeting, the result will be less fruitful. There is no buildup. You must always pre-schedule your quarterly meetings.

Many issues come up in the quarterly meetings that don't typically come up in the course of day-to-day business. Countless times, when a touchy subject comes up in the quarterly meeting that has been lingering, others will ask, "Why did you wait until today to bring it up?" Often they don't know why. It's because of the buildup. It has spurred thoughts beyond the routine. People are more focused, energetic, and ready.

THE WEEKLY MEETING PULSE

The traction process continues taking the vision down to the ground. We are now narrowing in from quarterly to weekly. Implementing this step will really create traction and help you execute the vision. Once the quarterly priorities are set, you must meet on a weekly basis to stay focused, solve issues, and communicate. As you can see by the following model, the Weekly Meeting Pulse is your opportunity to make sure that everything is on track. If you're on track for the week, then you're on track for the quarter, and if you're on track for the quarter, then you're on track for the year, and so on. The Meeting Pulse, like a heartbeat, creates a consistent flow that keeps the company healthy. Put another way, the Meeting Pulse creates a consistent cadence that keeps the organization in step.

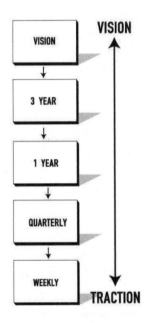

ALWAYS A LEVEL 10 MEETING

How would you rate your meetings on a scale from 1 to 10? The response is almost always somewhere between a 4 and a 5. That is simply not good enough. Most meetings in business are weak and not very productive, and yours probably are too. By implementing the ingredients of the Level 10 Meeting, you will raise that rating up to a 10.

The Level 10 Meeting Agenda is designed to keep your leadership team focused on what's most important on a weekly basis. Nothing is more important than keeping your numbers on track, your Rocks on track, and your customers and employees happy. The Level 10 Meeting is the most effective and efficient way to accomplish that.

A weekly Level 10 Meeting keeps you focused on what's important, helps you spot developing problems, and then drives you to solve them. What makes for great meetings is solving problems. Patrick Lencioni says it best: "Your meetings should be passionate, intense, exhausting, and never boring."

The Level 10 Meeting was developed as a result of being engaged by a number of clients to improve their meetings. The guiding principles are based on human nature. This agenda was developed through real-world trial and error and experimentation with many different methodologies. Today, all EOS clients follow this exact agenda.

THE EOS WEEKLY MEETING PULSE

Who: The leadership team

Where: The office conference room

Duration: 90 minutes

Frequency: Every Week

Prework: Rocks established and Rock Sheet created; Scorecard complete; Issues Solving Track understood by everyone

THE LEVEL 10 WEEKLY MEETING AGENDA

Segue	5 minutes
Scorecard	5 minutes
Rock review	5 minutes
Customer/employee headlines	5 minutes

To-Do List	5 minutes
IDS	60 minutes
Conclude	5 minutes

Two roles are vital in the Level 10 Meeting. One person must run the meeting. This person will move the team through the agenda and keep them on track. Second, someone must manage the agenda. This person makes sure that the agenda, Scorecard, and Rock Sheet are updated and in front of everyone in each meeting. They update the To-Do and Issues Lists in the agenda each week.

Segue

The meeting starts promptly. Football coach Vince Lombardi was famous for his mantra that early is on time, and on time is late. Arrive a few minutes early so you can start to get your head in the game. The only reasons for missing the weekly Level 10 Meeting are vacation or death. Even if someone cannot make the meeting, the show must go on. Don't reschedule it and don't cancel it.

Everyone should have a copy of the agenda placed in front of them. Your to-dos and your IDS Issues List should be included in the actual printed agenda. Your agenda should fit on one sheet so that you're only managing one piece of paper. You no longer need to take meeting minutes. They should be a thing of the past. If you want to know what was covered in a meeting, check that week's agenda.

As a team, you share good news to segue into the meeting. As always, you need to create the transition from working in the business all week to working on the business, disconnecting from day-to-day affairs. It's important to turn off all electronic devices so you can disconnect, take a deep breath, change gears, and get to work. In addition, the segue reminds you that you are all simply human beings in this world trying to create something great. This item should take no more than five minutes.

Scorecard

The Scorecard review is the leadership team's opportunity at a high level to examine the five to 15 most important numbers in the organization and to make sure they are on track for the goal. Any numbers that are not on track are dropped to the IDS portion of the meeting, which is your Issues List. Avoid any discussion here. The reporting phase should merely identify problem areas. The biggest pitfall with most teams is that they launch right into discussing and trying to solve an issue. You must fight that urge and be disciplined. That keeps the meeting on track. There will be plenty of time to discuss and solve issues in the IDS phase, and the process will be much more productive when you're addressing all of the issues at once. Scorecard review should take no more than 5 minutes.

Rock Review

Next, your leadership team focuses on your Rocks to make sure that they are on track. Review each Rock one at a time—first the company Rocks and then each person's individual Rocks. Each person reports that his or her Rock is either "on track" or "off track." No discussion—the discussion will happen later. When a Rock is off track, it's dropped to the IDS portion of the agenda. "On track" simply means that the owner of the Rock feels he or she will accomplish it by the end of the quarter. Even if a Rock is on track but someone wants an update or has a concern, it should be dropped to IDS. Rock review should take no more than 5 minutes.

Customer/Employee Headlines

Share short and sweet headlines about any customer or employee news or issues for the week, either good or bad. For example, "Joe, our best client, is happy with the job we did last week," or "Darla is upset with the decision on the new benefits program." The good news is a time to pat yourself on the back. Any issues, bad news, or concerns should be dropped to the IDS portion of the agenda. Some companies have a formal customer and/or employee feedback system. If your organization does, this is where you would incorporate that tool. Headlines should take no more than 5 minutes.

To-Do List

Review all to-dos from last week's meeting. To-dos are seven-day action items. From a weekly review comes accountability. By incorporating this agenda item, you will accomplish more as a team. To distinguish a Rock from a to-do, remember that a Rock is a 90-day priority while a to-do is a seven-day action item. To-dos consist of the commitments people make throughout the week that typically don't get captured. For example, "I'll call the printers tomorrow," "It will be shipped tonight," or "I will have every prospect on the list contacted by Friday."

Quickly review each item on the To-Do List from a standpoint of "done" or "not done." If the to-do is done, strike it from the list. If it's not done, leave it on the list. Note: An action item should not remain on the To-Do List for more than two weeks, and 90 percent of them should drop off every week.

The to-dos hold your team accountable to all the commitments they made in the previous week. All human beings are procrastinators by nature. Imagine what it would be like if everyone in your organization did everything they said they would. It would be a different world, right? The power of the To-Do List is uncanny. During the experimentation with running a client's weekly meetings, I discovered that the commitments that team members were making to each other from the previous week were not being carried out. People would make promises, such as making a call, shipping a package, or finishing a report. A week later, I would find that, of 10 commitments, only a few were done. As a result, I incorporated a To-Do List into the meeting. Once everyone had to report on them the following week, the number of tasks completed went from a few out of 10 to nine out of 10. Productivity increased because people knew they were going to be held accountable.

Traction and accountability are created when these weekly commitments are captured on the To-Do List and are reviewed for completion the following week. The days of making a commitment, knowing that no one is going to confirm that it was done, quickly fade. This agenda item should take less than 5 minutes.

IDS

This is where the magic happens. It's time to tackle your Issues List. Great meetings are created by solving problems. You should have 60 minutes for solving issues. This part should always take up most of your meeting.

On average, about three to five issues on the list will come from last week's meeting. During the reporting this week, you will have added new issues—about five to 10, on average. Typically, the list contains five to 15 issues. Although your Issues List is in your agenda, it can be effective to write your Issues List on a whiteboard or flip chart so it's in front of everyone. Many clients have said that this leads to better participation than everyone looking down at their copies of the agenda.

Decide which issues are number one, two, and three. Start with only the top three because, as a rule of thumb, you don't know how many you'll resolve. As long as you take them in order of priority, you're attacking the right ones. To repeat, it's a mistake to start at the top of the list and work your way down because sometimes the most important issue is near the bottom of the list. In addition, when you solve the most important issue, you tend to find out some of the other issues on the Issues List were symptoms of that core issue, and they drop off automatically.

Go to work on number one, and work on it alone until it's solved following the Issues Solving Track. Some weeks, you will get through only one issue. Other weeks, you will get through 10. You never know, but again, as long as you're taking them in order of priority, you're tackling the company's largest obstacles.

Once the issue has been identified, discussed, and solved, the solution usually turns into a plan of attack that ends up on the To-Do List. You may end up with one, two, or three to-dos as a result of that one solution. In next week's meeting, you will confirm that the to-dos have been accomplished and the problem has been solved forever, rather than hanging around as in the past.

Following the Issues Solving Track keeps a team focused on what's important, and it avoids spending time on what some may think is a priority and really isn't. This vital portion of the meeting should be passionate, intense, exhausting, and never boring. There should be no politics; the discussion should be open and honest, with everyone sharing the vision and fighting for the greater good. By solving all of your key issues for the week, you feel a tremendous sense of resolve and accomplishment.

Conclude

With five minutes left, move to conclude the meeting. This is your opportunity to pull the whole meeting together. You can frame everything that was discussed and make sure no loose ends are left.

Concluding has two parts. First, recap your new To-Do List. Quickly restate all of the action items on the list to confirm that everyone has theirs written down. This step reinforces accountability. Second, discuss whether any messages need to be communicated to the organization based on decisions you made today, how you're going to communicate them, and what medium you're going to use. This step will greatly reduce communication issues that may have occurred in the past, when people were surprised with changes that were made without their knowledge.

> I highly recommend adding a third item to your conclusion of the meeting to help you get instant feedback on how you're doing. Simply have everyone rate the meeting at the end on a scale of 1 to 10. Your goal should be an 8 or better.

At the end of the meeting, there should be a feeling of conclusion. The meeting ends on time. This avoids any domino effect where meetings run over and push other appointments back, blowing up people's schedules. And that is the Level 10 Meeting Agenda in a nutshell.

THE FIVE POINTS OF THE WEEKLY MEETING PULSE

A productive Meeting Pulse should meet the following five criteria. The meetings must

1. be on the same day each week,
2. be at the same time each week,
3. have the same printed agenda,
4. start on time, and
5. end on time.

Making the meeting the same day and time creates a routine. Using the same agenda discourages reinventing the wheel; once you have an agenda that works, stick to it. Plus, it also helps to keep the meetings consistent. Start on time, because when you start the meeting late, the part of the meeting that always suffers is the issues-solving time, and that's what matters most in the meeting. You will cut down the best part. And end on time so that you don't push back any following meetings.

LEVEL 10 WEEKLY MEETING AGENDA*

SEGUE	**5 min**
SCORECARD	**5 min**
ROCK REVIEW	**5 min**
CUSTOMER/EMPLOYEE HEADLINES	**5 min**
TO-DO LIST	**5 min**

      • John to call ABC Co.
      • Bill to have a meeting with Sara
      • Sue will call the supplier
      • Jack to revise core values speech

IDS	**60 min**

      • Winter sales are down
      • We missed the delivery date on ABC
      • A/R is over 60 days
      • Charles is not following the process

CLOSE	**5 min**

Notice how the to-dos and issues are built right into the agenda.

Be patient with the Weekly Meeting Pulse. Your first meeting will be awkward, but as you stay committed to it, it will become very comfortable. The level of team health, communication, and results will consistently rise.

THE WEEKLY MEETING ROLLOUT

Once you master the Weekly Meeting Pulse as a leadership team, the next step is to roll it out to each department. Clients typically take about three months to institute the Weekly Meeting Pulse throughout their organization, because the leadership team must master it first. Departmental weekly meetings are typically closer to 30 to 60 minutes. Use the Level 10 Meeting Agenda as a guide for customizing your departmental meeting agendas. Just make sure that at least 50 percent of the meeting time is spent solving issues.

MEETING PULSE ACTIONS

1. **Schedule your quarterly session as close to the quarter's end as possible and then every quarter after that.** Follow the agenda and Rock-setting process in your quarterly meetings, then roll Rocks out by department.

2. **Decide when your Weekly Meeting Pulse will be as a leadership team.** Pick the ideal day and time for you to meet every week. There is no rule of thumb; just decide what works best for you.

3. **Follow the Level 10 Meeting to the letter for one month.** At the end of the month, read this chapter again. Make any fine-tuning adjustments, and then continue for another month. If in the future you find yourself getting off track again, refer back to the chapter as often as necessary to stay focused.

4. **Decide who is going to run the meeting.** There can only be one. This person has to be comfortable moving people along and pushing them through the agenda when they are getting off track.

5. **Decide who is going to manage the agenda.** This person keeps the To-Do and Issues Lists updated during the meeting and makes sure a copy of the agenda, the Rock Sheet, and the Scorecard are placed in front of everyone when the meeting starts every week.

By setting Rocks and implementing a Meeting Pulse that creates a 90-Day World and weekly focus, you gain tremendous traction toward your vision.

You are now doing what the successful companies do. Your frustrations from the past start to subside, and you make progress on your way to breaking through the ceiling. Your organization evolves from chaotic to a well-oiled machine. Your journey is now complete. Or has it just started?

THE TRACTION COMPONENT

ROCKS

- The three to seven most important things that must get done in the next 90 days
- The Rock Sheet
- Everyone should have Rocks

MEETING PULSE

- The 90-Day World
- Annuals and quarterlies
- Weekly Level 10 Meetings
- Same day and time each week; same printed agenda; start on time and end on time

CHAPTER 9

PULLING IT
ALL TOGETHER

THE GRAND JOURNEY

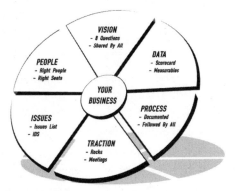

N ow that the context is clear, mastery of all Six Key Components is within reach. You're well on your way to achieving 100 percent. Mastery means that you and your leadership team understand each tool and have implemented them properly.

Many books have been written on the topics of meetings, planning, solving problems, developing people, and prioritizing. What is new about the Entrepreneurial Operating System (EOS) is the way these disciplines have been assembled into a complete system for running an entrepreneurial organization. Each individual tool is not as important as the whole, and all six components that make up the Entrepreneurial Operating System and The EOS Model need to be understood and mastered in order to fully gain traction.

If, as many clients do, you want a visual of The EOS Model in front of you to serve as a constant reminder of the Six Key Components, you can download one free at **www.eosworldwide.com/model**.

The combination of strengthening the Vision, People, Data, Issues, Process, and Traction Components is what makes the real magic occur. This book started from the premise that, whether consciously or unconsciously, successful entrepreneurs have a habit of strengthening six components of their business, and to the degree that you can do so yourself, you will build a great organization. As a result, your frustrations regarding control of your time and your business will diminish. Frustrations about employees will fall away because you will be surrounded by the right people in the right seats. You will finally break through the ceiling you've been hitting, you will transform your everyday business, and, ultimately, you will realize your organization's vision. At this point, I hope that you now see that premise is true.

As your leadership team works toward implementing these tools, you may have trouble seeing progress. The results won't always show on your P&L right away. In the early stages, you're also going to dredge up a lot of issues that will feel a bit overwhelming. Rosabeth Moss Kanter, Harvard Business School professor and bestselling author of *Confidence: How Winning and Losing Streaks Begin and End*, once described what she refers to as Kanter's law: "Everything can look like a failure in the middle." Sometimes on your journey, you'll feel like it's not working. When this occurs, I urge you to stay the course. Mastery requires total commitment, and gaining traction requires a complete operating system.

Shifting your organization from chaos to strengthening the Six Key Components was the journey to this point. It's now time to take a little pressure off, because achieving 100 percent requires a state of perfection that doesn't exist. Truth be told, if you can reach even 80 percent, you will have a great company. That's because the work of managing an EOS company is never complete and never automatic. Just like the task of keeping anything else healthy, it takes nurturing, care, and a maintained routine.

Anything you learn from now on regarding running and building a great business will fit into this context, The EOS Model. Your challenge will be deciding which ones align with the greater good of your company and which ones don't. Always let your core values, core focus, and 10-year target be your guide.

I recommend that you and your leadership team fill out the Organizational Checkup together at least twice a year to see how you're progressing. This will give you a snapshot of where you are on the journey between zero and 100 percent. The goal is that you are always making progress.

The real goal is 80 percent or better. If you're above that level, you have a well-oiled machine with the traction you require. The highest score ever achieved is 88 percent, by The Benefits Company, a 10-person organization that is one of the best small companies I've ever seen. Rob Tamblyn, the owner and a pure visionary, had a vision to create the best service company in the benefits business.

Since beginning The EOS Process, The Benefits Company has experienced 30 percent growth on average every year for the last five years. To say that it's gaining traction would be an understatement.

Filling out the Organizational Checkup at least twice every year shows you how you're progressing as an organization. Together with your leadership team, you can find the gaps between where you are and where you want to go. The gaps are issues that go on the Issues List. You can then determine if they are a high enough priority to tackle. If so, the solutions become goals, Rocks, and to-dos for the coming year.

For example, say you rate yourselves a 3 out of 5 on the fifth statement, "Our target market is clear, and our sales and marketing efforts are focused on it." You might decide that a Rock for this quarter is for the sales manager to redefine your target market, clean up your sales pipeline, and train all salespeople on it.

Another example might be that you rated yourselves a 4 out of 5 on the first statement, "We have a clear vision in writing that has been properly communicated and shared by everyone." You realize the gap is that not everyone shares the vision and you have not been sharing it often enough. As a result you set a Rock for the quarter to address several people who do not share the vision and to make a decision on their future. In addition, someone has a to-do to schedule a meeting with everyone to share the vision again and get back on track with quarterly company meetings.

ORGANIZATIONAL CHECKUP

For each statement below, rank your business on a scale of 1 to 5 where 1 is weak and 5 is strong.

	1 2 3 4 5
1. We have a clear vision in writing that has been properly communicated and is shared by everyone.	
2. Our core values are clear, and we are hiring, reviewing, rewarding, and firing around them.	

3. Our core business is clear, and our systems and processes reflect that.

4. Our 10-year target is clear and has been communicated to everyone.

5. Our target market is clear, and our sales and marketing efforts are focused on it.

6. Our differentiators are clear, and all of our sales and marketing efforts communicate them.

7. We have a proven process for doing business with our customers. It has been named and visually illustrated, and everyone is adhering to it.

8. All of the people in our organization are the right people.

9. Our Accountability Chart (organizational chart of roles and responsibilities) is clear, complete, and constantly updated.

10. Everyone is in the right seat.

11. Our leadership team is open and honest, and demonstrates a high level of trust.

12. Everyone has Rocks and is focused on them (3 to 7 priorities per quarter).

13. Everyone is engaged in regular weekly meetings.

14. All meetings are on the same day and at the same time each week, have the same printed agenda, start on time, and end on time.

15. All teams clearly identify, discuss, and solve key issues for the greater good and long term.

☐ ☐ ☐ ☐ ☐

16. Our systems and processes are documented, simplified, and followed by all.

☐ ☐ ☐ ☐ ☐

17. We have a system for receiving regular customer and employee feedback, and we know their level of satisfaction.

☐ ☐ ☐ ☐ ☐

18. A Scorecard for weekly metrics and measurables is in place.

☐ ☐ ☐ ☐ ☐

19. Everyone in the organization has a number.

☐ ☐ ☐ ☐ ☐

20. We have a budget and are monitoring it regularly (i.e., monthly or quarterly).

☐ ☐ ☐ ☐ ☐

Total number of each ranking

☐ ☐ ☐ ☐ ☐

Multiply by the number above

×1 ×2 ×3 ×4 ×5

☐ ☐ ☐ ☐ ☐

Add all five numbers to determine the percentage score that reflects the current state of your company: ☐ %.

One more example might be that you rated yourselves 2 out of 5 on statement number 16: "Our systems and processes are documented, simplified, and followed by all." Seeing this gap, you agree as a team once and for all to make it a goal for this year to finally document your core processes.

Filling out the Organizational Checkup at least twice every year will clarify all gaps, put those issues into action, and ultimately enable you to continue to climb toward 100 percent. The goal is progress, not perfection. You might feel frustrated because you're not at 88 percent like the Benefits Company. Yet success is not based on where you are, but on how far you have come. If you were at 55 percent last year and at 63 percent this year, that's success. The next year you'll be at 72 percent and maybe 80 percent in the year after that. Keep using the principles, and you'll break through.

DISCOVERIES, POTHOLES, AND DELAYS ON THE GRAND JOURNEY

ROLLING OUT EOS TO YOUR COMPANY

Once your leadership team has mastered the tools in The EOS Process, it's time to roll out the tools to the rest of the organization. This is best done one tier at a time. At first, introduce the tools only to the people who report to the leadership team. If you're a 10-person company, that would cover everyone. But if you're a 250-person company, you'll go through a couple of tiers before you get to everyone. When rolling the tools out, I recommend first choosing what are known as foundational tools. These are as follows:

- The V/TO
- The Accountability Chart
- Rocks
- The Meeting Pulse
- The Scorecard

The other tools will follow in the order of priority that you establish as a leadership team based on the organization's current state and issues.

YOU CAN ONLY MOVE AT YOUR OWN SPEED

Be patient with this process. I originally believed I could advance every company through the process at the same speed. In Month One, the Accountability Chart would be completed. In Month Two, the perfect leadership team would be in place. In Month Three, everyone would have mastered Rocks and created a solid Meeting Pulse. By the end of Month Six, all processes would be documented. After many years, I have come to realize that this goal is unrealistic. Each company moves forward at its own pace. Forcing it to move any faster could be damaging.

Two EOS clients from different ends of the spectrum make this point clear. Without giving names, the first client made two key leadership team changes in the first three months of the process. That means he removed two key people from the organization and replaced them in 90 days. That is a blinding speed. The second client took two and a half years to make the first change on his team, and after four years, he has yet to make the second. This is not a criticism. If I pushed him any faster, it would actually be detrimental. He must feel ready to make the decision. In the meantime, the company is still growing at about 8 percent per year.

The other determining factor of how fast you can move is the current state of the company and the number of people in it. It takes longer to turn a large ship than a small one. A 200-person organization is going to take longer to change than a 15-person organization. If you have to turn over 50 percent of your people, the process will take longer than if you have to turn over 10 percent.

McKinley is a textbook example of rollout. Keep in mind that McKinley is a 700-person company, one of the largest real estate investment and property management companies in the United States. Upon completing our first few sessions, the leadership team went to work on rolling out the foundational tools (V/TO, Accountability Chart, Rocks, Meeting Pulse, and Scorecard) one tier at a time. A full year passed before the tools were understood and implemented by every person in the organization. In Year Two, they documented, simplified, and trained everyone in their core processes—their common platform, as they called it. Year Three saw them rolling out a measurable for everyone and educating each person on how he or she contributes to the company's financial success, while tying compensation to it. Each year CEO Albert Berriz defined the right focus for the company and exercised discipline with flawless consistency. Three years might seem like a long time, but McKinley is a big ship. To see how far they have come in three short years is remarkable. If your ship is smaller, you may be able to make the transition faster.

One of the fastest companies to roll out the tools was Professional Grounds Services. It's a 100-employee landscape and snow-removal company that does large office and industrial projects. It rolled out the foundational tools in less than a year. In that time, Professional Grounds Services shared its V/TO with everyone, implemented a new structure, removed a key person from the leadership team, gave everyone a number, and ensured its processes were being documented and followed. Nowadays, the company tears through issues with the best of them. It's a true case study in efficient execution.

WHY IT WORKS

The reason EOS works in any kind of organization is that it's based on human nature. The entire system is built around how people really operate:

- **The 90-Day World** stems from the reality that humans can only focus that long.

- **The To-Do List** in the weekly meeting is designed to ensure accountability. When people know someone is going to check up on what they committed to, they do it.

- **The V/TO** is designed to get your vision out of your head and into the heads of others using a simplified approach of answering only eight questions. This makes it easier for people to see. When they can see it, they will believe it and it's more likely to happen.

- **Data** forces you to give people numbers so you can measure achievement. People relate to numbers because measuring is a natural human tendency. It creates a benchmark. If you create a culture in your sales department of attending two prospect appointments a week, people will strive to hit that mark. Setting measurable targets will direct their activity.

- **Core values** go to the heart of human nature. Like attracts like. People who are like-minded work well with each other. Different people have different values, but when you meet someone who has yours, there is an instant fit.

- **The Meeting Pulse** forces people to "keep the circles connected," as Sam Cupp would say. People need to stay connected. The saying "Out of sight, out of mind" is true in any company. If you don't stay connected, you're going to start to stray and people will start to work at cross-purposes.

- **The Issues Solving Track** addresses the natural tendency to avoid conflict, hoping that a problem will go away on its own. It won't, and by giving people a track to follow—IDS —they will solve it and feel better that they did.

- **A single system** directs talent and energy in one direction. It gets everyone speaking the same language and playing by the same rules. You move forward more quickly and everybody wins.

THE "CLICK"

At some point in the process comes the big "aha" moment when everyone gets it. Everything will "click" for your leadership team. They will see all the pieces of the puzzle come together and clearly understand how EOS is a complete system and why it works. One client, a premier marketing and communications company with clients such as General Motors, NBC Universal, Master Lock, and Stanley, had the big "click" exactly one year after starting the process. It was during the segue in a quarterly session.

While discussing what was working, the leadership team shared things such as, "Issues are being pushed down to the appropriate team and being solved," "We are making decisions with our core focus in mind," "Everyone is focused on Rocks that align with the company goals," and "I see how everyone being clear on and following the process is going to lead to better communication, fewer mistakes, and happier clients." That is the moment I live for. It's the lightbulb turning on. It will occur anywhere from the first six months to 36 months. I never know when it will happen, but when it does, the organization takes off from there.

YOU HAVE TO DO THE WORK

Don't think that your company will get better simply because you've read this book or attended an EOS session. You'll still need to do the work. You'll need to manage your people, talk to your clients, make tough decisions, and do all of the daily blocking and tackling that goes on inside a business. When Dan Israel of ASI realized after a year into the process that he and his team were suffering from neglecting the process, he shared this analogy: "It's like going to the doctor and not taking the medicine, thinking that going to the doctor is the cure." After Dan's realization, they sprang into real, meaningful action, and are now generating three times the profit as when they started the process. That's not because of me, but because they did the work.

STAY COMMITTED TO THE 90-DAY WORLD

Once you're on track, occasionally you or members of your leadership team will doubt the need for the quarterly meeting. Occasionally I have to explain to a client why he or she needs to hold the quarterly meetings when "everything is going well." At the end of the session, the client always says, "We really needed that." A quarterly meeting is essential whether things are going well or not. You'll need to keep everyone on the same page and make sure you're all on track for your vision by reviewing how you did last quarter and setting next quarter's Rocks. If you let a few quarters go by without the meetings, you will end up right back where you started. It's like taking your foot off of the gas pedal; you're not going to come to a screeching halt. You'll just coast until you eventually come to a stop.

Another common excuse to avoid meetings is that you're all too busy or that things are too chaotic. This is all the more reason to meet. Don't worry about what hasn't been accomplished. You must come together, assess where you are, reset, and take on the next quarter.

YOU WILL HIT THE CEILING AGAIN

As your numbers start to climb, you will actually feel a difference. You'll start to gain traction and move toward your vision. At some point, though, you will hit another ceiling. When this happens, you have to continue to practice the five leadership abilities. You have to:

1. Simplify, using the EOS tools. Remember that less is more. When everything is important, nothing is important.

2. Delegate and elevate by knowing when you and others are at capacity.

3. Predict well, both for the long term and short term, through your V/TO, Scorecard, and Rock setting and by following the Issues Solving Track.

4. Systemize by consistently managing your core processes.

5. Structure your organization the right way using the Accountability Chart, which continually evolves as you grow.

As a result of continuing to hone these five leadership abilities, you will break through the ceiling every time you hit it.

Niche Retail is a good example. When I started working with the company four years ago, it hit its first ceiling at around $4 million in revenue. Last year, it hit the ceiling again at $12 million. Niche Retail had to make a few changes to its structure and staff, which involved moving its entire customer service department from Minneapolis to Michigan. It also completely overhauled the finance department and implemented a new IT system organization-wide. As a result, it broke through again and is on track for $18 million in revenue this year. Just like Niche Retail, you too will grow until you hit another ceiling. If you're willing to stay disciplined and continually focus on the Six Key Components, you will break through the next one as well.

BIGGER ISN'T ALWAYS BETTER

As we said earlier, growth for growth's sake is normally a mistake. Being a $100-million company is not all it's cracked up to be. In *Good to Great*, Jim Collins alludes to the fact that we will never know the greatest company in America because it may be some $10-million business in Middle America that doesn't want to be known. You have to ask yourself this: Would you rather have a $10-million company with a 20 percent profit or a $100-million company with a 2 percent profit? It's the same net profit, with considerably more work at a higher complexity. The answer should be a no-brainer.

Don't get me wrong, though. There are great $100-million companies, even great $100-billion companies, but they're the exception, not the rule. Unless you have a really good reason to go to $100 million, why not become the best $10-million company there is?

After hitting their next ceiling at around $19 million and 70 people, Tyler Smith and his partner shocked their community (me included) by deciding to shut down Niche Retail.

In a very real, open, and honest interview with Tyler, I learned that the number one reason for his decision is that he felt he was no longer living in his Unique Ability. He felt the company had outgrown what he and his partner had wanted. They had ridden a wave of ego, hype, and excitement for nine years, and it had been a heck of a ride. "We were like rock stars at trade shows. It was intoxicating," Tyler says. "We got addicted to the money and the size." As he looks back, he remembers that Niche was supposed to be a lifestyle company but had grown too fast and they couldn't get out of their own way.

Tyler loves technology, computers, and the Internet. He found himself with 70 people at the helm of the company, in an industry he didn't like and in a role he didn't like. "I realized I no longer wanted to be an integrator," he says. He felt unfulfilled and bored. "To worsen matters, our industry was under attack by competitors like Wal-Mart, Amazon, and overfunded new companies. We also got hit with a recession; it was a triple whammy. I don't know what we would have done without the EOS tools on this ride. They're what held everything together."

Now, one year later, Tyler and his partner have started a new company that he feels puts them 100 percent in their Unique Abilites. Their company is called NicheNext and partners with companies to optimize their web sales. "I don't ever want to manage another employee," Tyler says. "I'm happier and more energized, and I'll make more money."

The message is that building a great organization isn't for everyone. Being an integrator isn't for everyone. You have to know what you want.

In his book *Small Giants: Companies That Choose to Be Great Instead of Big*, Bo Burlingham illustrates the value of staying small. He shares countless real-world stories of companies that chose to stay small and private. These companies shunned the chance to go public or receive unlimited amounts of money to invest in growth in order to protect and preserve what they'd built. They define themselves by their passion for their products and their commitment to their employees, customers, and community—by embracing a clarity and loyalty to their purpose.

COMPARTMENTALIZING

With EOS implemented, everything has its place. In other words, every issue, priority, action, or idea that is longer term than 90 days is listed on your V/TO Issues List. Anything that must be accomplished this year becomes a goal. If it needs to get done this quarter and will take weeks or months to accomplish, it becomes a Rock. Any issues that arise during the quarter and must be solved now go onto your weekly Level 10 leadership meeting Issues List. Issues that are departmental in nature get pushed down to the appropriate departmental meeting Issues List, and any that are one- to two-week action items go on the To-Do List in your Level 10 Meetings, creating a simple system for managing all goals, Rocks, issues, and to-dos.

SAME-PAGE MEETINGS

When you have a partnership, it's crucial for the greater good of the company, its culture, and people that the leadership is 100 percent on the same page. This also applies to all visionary/integrator relationships, even if they are not partnerships. When you're not in sync, your people will know it. As with parenting, the kids know when their parents are not getting along, as much as they try to hide it. The same goes with partners in business. In these situations, I prescribe a same-page meeting. Every month, you meet for a few hours and reconnect the circles. You need to solve all of your issues, share anything that is angering you, and express any concerns. These meetings are not always peaceful, but you will clear the air and resolve issues. The objective of the meeting is to communicate your thoughts, listen to the other's concerns, and solve all issues before bringing them into the business. You must also maintain a united front in front of all employees.

Take the example of Todd Sachse and his partner, Rich Broder. Early on in their process, I prescribed the same-page meeting for them, and they loved it. They have been holding same-page meetings every month for almost four years now, and their company has experienced explosive growth.

If you can't get on the same page, you might want to consider counseling or coaching. This practice is not uncommon, and mediation can be very effective. If you've tried everything and feel there is no hope, it may be time to part ways, although this is very rare. Generally, with counseling, you can get back on the same page, and the relationship will become better then ever.

I've had several clients end their partnerships after clarity of vision and accountability and discipline were put in place. Some partners just can't handle what it takes to build a strong company. If you're determined to go to the next level, some won't be ready for the change involved. Such a situation occurred with a new client when the decision to part ways occurred prior to completing three sessions. In the first session, it was apparent that the partnership no longer worked. The partners, who we'll call Jim and Tim, wanted two totally different environments. Jim wanted to keep the status quo, and Tim wanted to leave its chaos behind and build a solid company. In their second session, the vision was clarified solely by Tim, because Jim wanted nothing to do with it. Jim didn't even show up for the third. They had sat down after the second session and agreed to part ways.

The partners of a different company realized their diverging viewpoints in the first session, struggled through the second session, and cancelled the third session. They consulted their financial people and split up their assets into two separate companies. They now run their own companies as sole proprietors.

Even more complicated was a new potential client in which the partners were also brothers. When I entered the conference room for the initial meeting, I found only one brother waiting for me. He explained that after the meeting I would have to meet with the other brother down the hall and go through the exact same presentation. They wouldn't even sit in the same room together. So I did both meetings, more out of curiosity than anything else. As you can imagine, we never moved forward and any advice fell on deaf ears.

Fortunately, these painful partner situations occur only about 5 percent of the time. If you're faced with one, follow the same-page meeting process. If there is no hope, the answer is clear. Think about the long-term view, and you will see that by separating you will be better off in the long run.

TAKE A CLARITY BREAK

Keeping your head clear, your confidence high, and your focus strong are vital in maintaining forward momentum. Most leaders spend most of their time overwhelmed, tired, and buried in the day-to-day routine, unable to see beyond tomorrow. As a result, they don't solve problems as well as they could, they don't lead their people as well as they could, and they're not a good example for them.

Great leaders have a habit of taking quiet thinking time. That means escaping the office on a regular basis for an hour or so. By working on yourself and the business, you will rise above feeling frustrated and overwhelmed to a clearheaded and confident state. As a result, when you come back into the business, you will be laser-focused and in the right leadership frame of mind.

You can do this wherever works best for you; it should never be in your office. You have to go to a place where your thoughts are uninterrupted. You can do this daily, weekly, or monthly, whichever works best for you. Some clients have a favorite place in the morning on the way to work. Sam Cupp would do it 30 minutes in his den every morning. I do it once a week for two hours in a coffee shop. I knew a man that would take about half a day every month at the library, and that did the trick for him.

Such free time to think is vital. As Henry Ford said, "Thinking is the hardest work there is, which is probably the reason why so few engage in it." Take the opportunity to review your V/TO, review your plans, read, think strategically, look at The EOS Model, or fill out the Organizational Checkup. What I recommend for someone that doesn't know what to do is to sit with a blank legal pad and a pen. I promise you, through this simple exercise, all of the right thoughts will come to mind. It's important that none of the work you're doing is busy work. This is not an opportunity for playing catch-up.

After taking a clarity break, you will come back into the business clear, focused, and confident. You'll be ready for anything. You'll solve problems better, you'll be clearer with your people, and you'll set a better example. When you're having trouble solving a problem, check out for a clarity break. Take a deep breath, and put the necessary time into thinking clearly through the problem.

To start, pick a one-hour block of time next week, block it out, and do it. If you wait around for the right time to appear, it never will. It must be an appointment that you schedule with yourself. Give it a try. Just do one. I have yet to have one person tell me that it was a waste of time. You might be wondering where you're going to find an hour. The amazing paradox is that the hour you spend will save you more than that hour later due to the clarity that it creates. You end up being much more efficient and effective.

SHINY STUFF

When the business is really humming and on track, you may get a little fidgety and start to get distracted by shiny stuff. This mostly happens to visionaries. Here are two discipline strategies to keep you focused and engaged.

First, find a challenge inside the business. Focus on your "acres of diamonds." Put your energy into something that is going to perpetuate the existing vision. Dive into cultural projects that will boost the core values and the people. Experiment with some new products or services in line with the company's core focus. Go interview your top clients and really dig into what is working and what is not working for them. Take employees to lunch and ask them the same kind of questions. Test current products and services, and make sure they are still relevant. All of these activities will keep you stimulated and further the vision of the company.

Second, if you're starting to become distracted by shiny stuff that is outside your core focus and your leadership is supportive, then go explore. You must, however, protect your existing business, making sure the integrator is comfortable with your reduced time commitment. You cannot drain any necessary resources or energy that the current company needs to achieve its vision. If your new business idea is a good one, and it doesn't fit in the current core focus, consider starting a new company with its own resources. Too many times, a new idea is incorporated into the current company, and it's the kiss of death, due to stretched resources such as people, cash, and time. Even when both are great business ideas, they are destined to fail when they do not have the resources they need.

StarTrax, a social event company that provides entertainment for parties and events, is a good example. Along the way, they stumbled into corporate event planning, which demands a different clientele, culture, and model. Nonetheless, they decided to pursue it. After flat growth and struggling to run two businesses in one over a three-year period, they realized it was time to separate the two. The dual-headed company was creating too much complexity and draining its resources. They found an integrator to run the social business, made him a partner, and then separated it. They suddenly had two very focused businesses with an integrator at the helm of each one. StarTrax is now running well and growing. The second company has been renamed pulse220 and has grown 40 percent each of the last two years.

If you're getting distracted by shiny stuff, choose one discipline and stick with it.

THE ROAD TO HANA

Some time ago, a friend of mine and his wife visited a major Maui tourist attraction called The Road to Hana. It comprised a long and winding road that, over the course of hours, took them through breathtaking scenery, waterfalls, cliffs, mountains, and beaches. At the end, there was nothing but the small town of Hana, with one gas station. When they finally arrived, my friend's wife was very upset. She said, "We drove all of this way for this?" She missed the point. The Road to Hana is about the journey, not the destination.

Don't make the same mistake with The EOS Process. The journey of building a great business is not about the destination at all. Of course, you want it to be highly profitable and generate wealth for yourself and others. Yet, along the way, you need to enjoy the lives that you'll touch. You need to get excited about the value you'll create for customers, enjoy the pure pleasure of playing the game of business, and be able to take pride in the self-perpetuating system you've built. Once you have created a business that doesn't require you to crank every single gear—an entity all its own—you'll have more freedom for yourself. The journey should be enjoyable. If you're racing to get to the end of the journey, you'll be sorely disappointed.

By embracing this journey-focused approach, you're going against the grain of what most believe is right. As a result, it's hard to understand the truth. As Tal Ben-Shahar, PhD, states in his book *Happier: Learn the Secrets to Daily Joy and Lasting Fulfillment*, "Society rewards results, not processes; arrivals, not journeys." The irony is that if you're able to fight society's pull, you will then enjoy all of the journey's rewards.

My closing on all my correspondence is "Stay focused." If every person could just do that, they would be happier and more successful. We live in a world that inundates us with information. There is so much shiny stuff that it's hard to concentrate. If I could leave you with one message, it's that: Stay focused. As for what to focus on, that's your decision. It all starts with answering the eight questions.

Chapter 10

Getting
STARTED

A t this point, you're probably eager to put these tools to work in your organization. To help you get the fastest results in the shortest amount of time, I'll outline the exact process that I use to implement each EOS tool with our clients. Ultimately, these will strengthen the Six Key Components.

The objective of this book is to teach the Six Key Components and the tools that will strengthen each of them. It's written in a specific order using The EOS Model, basically top to bottom and right to left, in an attempt to keep the learning and understanding as linear as possible. While this is the best way to write this book and create understanding, the most effective order of implementation of each tool is different.

The objective of this chapter is to provide the exact steps in order. Following this process has proven to be the most efficient way to get the fastest results. Keep in mind that you can implement them in any order you choose, but I highly recommend you go straight down the list.

You might want to first check the overview of The EOS Process on page 63. After hands-on implementation with over 120 companies personally and an additional 300 with our team of implementers, I've learned the most effective way to proceed. I will first share the tool in the sequence and then the reason for that order. I won't get into the specific how-tos, as they're already explained in the earlier chapters.

You've learned a total of seven main tools in this book, with an additional 12 secondary supportive tools. Each stands on its own, but when they're combined, you have a complete and holistic system for running your organization. As I've mentioned before, I suggest you implement each of the following tools only within your leadership team first. Make sure you and your leadership team have mastered them before rolling them out to the rest of your organization. Any chink in the armor of your leadership team will show up as a gaping rip to the rest of your people, so this step is vital. Once your team has fully embraced them, I'll show you how to introduce them to the rest of your company.

The seven main tools are listed in the order of recommended implementation, along with the 12 secondary tools that go with them:

1. Accountability Chart (which includes People Analyzer and GWC)

2. Rocks

3. Meeting Pulse (which includes IDS, Level 10 Meeting, Quarterlies, and Annuals)

4. Scorecard

5. V/TO (which includes core values, core focus, 10-year target, marketing strategy, three-year picture, and one-year plan)

6. Three-Step Process Documenter

7. Everyone Has a Number

ACCOUNTABILITY CHART (WHICH INCLUDES PEOPLE ANALYZER AND GWC)

Begin by creating your Accountability Chart. The reason we start here with every client is that the chart goes to the root of most issues. First, you need to take a big step back and determine the right structure for your organization. Then you can put the right people in the right seats. Through this initial strategy, you will smoke out any people and accountability issues that are holding you back.

When complete, you'll have absolute clarity on who is accountable for what. If this tool is set in place before you apply the remaining tools, they'll be much more potent and effective because you'll have created a world of accountability. For instance, with a completed Accountability Chart in place, you'll draw up your V/TO with your leadership team with a more complete, realistic vision and plan for your organization. Without an Accountability Chart, you won't know who clearly owns what. In this environment, teams tend to shoot a little higher, and there's less productive discussion and debate due to increased bravado and lack of true ownership.

ROCKS

Once your Accountability Chart is complete, you should move to the second tool: setting Rocks. Once you know who is accountable for what, you set better Rocks. You want your team to evolve toward setting and achieving great Rocks every 90 days. The other reason Rocks are the second tool to implement is that it focuses your team on the most important priorities quickly and gets you to work on accomplishing them.

The reality is that the first time around, you will set mediocre Rocks and only achieve about 50 percent of them. This has been historically accurate for over 10 years with our clients. Within two or three quarters of setting and achieving Rocks, though, you and your team will become experts at Rock setting and achieving, accomplishing a minimum of 80 percent collectively each quarter.

MEETING PULSE (WHICH INCLUDES IDS, LEVEL 10 MEETING, QUARTERLIES, AND ANNUALS)

With your Accountability Chart in place and your leadership team laser-focused on their Rocks, the third tool to implement is the Meeting Pulse, specifically the 90-minute weekly Level 10 Meeting. This new habit is a bit uncomfortable at first. You'll probably take four to eight weeks to really become comfortable with it. Still, the tool forces your team to single out what's important every week and start solving the right problems.

Implementing the weekly Level 10 Meeting relies on the proper use of one of the secondary tools, IDS. The Level 10 Meeting forces you to use this tool to identify, discuss, and solve all relevant issues. This will help you gain immediate traction.

As for your quarterly and annual meeting pulse, you simply start those based on where you are in the calendar year.

SCORECARD

With momentum building, the fourth main tool to implement is the Scorecard. You need to develop your Scorecard into a powerful predictive tool, a process that takes one to three months. Soon you and your team will have an absolute pulse on your business. During this developmental process, you will create real accountability as you identify the right activity-based numbers to measure and clearly identify the person who ultimately owns the number. This will create instant results and ownership.

V/TO (WHICH INCLUDES CORE VALUES, CORE FOCUS, 10-YEAR TARGET, MARKETING STRATEGY, THREE-YEAR PICTURE, AND ONE-YEAR PLAN)

The first four main tools create a strong foundation of traction, accountability, and a platform from which to execute your vision. That leads to the fifth tool, the V/TO. One of the secrets to The EOS Process is that we always start with traction first and then vision. This means that we first build a strong foundation for execution with the first four main tools, then we build the vision. Frankly, the vision work is relatively simple when there is little or no discipline and accountability. Without a nuts-and-bolts foundation, devising a vision is easy. That's why it's so fun for many consultants who spend their time doing two-day strategic planning sessions.

Doing the tough work of putting a strong foundation of accountability in place leads to much more intense and productive planning work. You can have great discussions of what the *right* plan is for the organization, because your people are now being measured and held fully accountable for the objectives of the company.

Still, a question I'm often asked is, "How can you create an Accountability Chart and set Rocks before you know what your vision is?" The truth is, most organizations have a pretty good idea where they're going already. After all, they're not exactly starting from scratch.

The real questions to ask are these: How are you going to get the best bang for your buck with these tools? Where will you get the most impact in the shortest period of time? What I've learned over the last decade with over 400 companies is that this approach is it.

THE EOS FOUNDATIONAL TOOLS

The Accountability Chart, Rocks, Meeting Pulse, Scorecard, and V/TO are known as the EOS foundational tools. Implementing them into your entire company produces 80 percent of the results. As you expand the use of these tools, it's important to introduce them one tier at a time until each person in that tier understands and embraces them, just as we did with the leadership team.

Every company moves at its own pace. Our fastest client, a 50-person organization, rolled out the foundational tools from top to bottom in six months. In contrast, our slowest client, a 70-person company, needed over three years. Neither is bad or good—you can only move as fast as you're able to absorb the changes. A good rule of thumb is about a year. Also, a larger company will take longer than a smaller company. By the same token, a company with more tiers (layers) takes longer than a company with less. To date, our smallest client has three people and our largest has 1,700.

One important note for companies with multiple locations: It's vital that the manager at the off-site location fully embraces and understands each foundational tool before rolling them out to the next tier in his or her location. Many times, leadership team members need to be present at locations to help teach, guide, and show support for the tools. So, if you have multiple locations, it adds an inherent level of complexity to your organization. It's just the reality of your business model. Accepting this reality is the first step to solving it. Plan on spending the necessary time at these locations until full implementation is achieved. This additional time can be achieved through physical visits, conference calls, and webinars. All have worked well with our clients, and every company is different in terms of which approach works best.

THREE-STEP PROCESS DOCUMENTER

When you have the foundational tools fully implemented in your entire company and everyone is clear and has bought into them, the next step is documenting and training your core processes using the sixth main tool, the Three-Step Process Documenter. This is typically a six- to 12-month process, including documentation and fully training everyone.

One additional note is that some clients do begin implementing this tool prior to full implementation of the foundational tools. A simple rule of thumb is that if you feel you're on track with the implementation of the previous tools and your leadership team has the capacity, then go ahead and overachieve by getting a jump start on implementing this tool.

EVERYONE HAS A NUMBER

The seventh and final main tool is that everyone must have a number. With most of our clients, this is the last domino to fall. While a highly effective tool, without the first six main tools in place, it's less effective due to a lack of follow-through that stems from a lack of accountability, discipline, and strong management. However, with a strong foundation in place, everyone having a number in your organization gives you increased results.

ONGOING IMPLEMENTATION AND REINFORCEMENT

Once the above seven main tools are implemented along with the additional 12 supportive tools, it's important to know what ongoing implementation, reinforcement, and management look like, because getting your head around all the tools at once is a lot and can get overwhelming.

Here's a snapshot: Imagine all of the above-mentioned tools fully implemented. Every quarter, you're in a full-day quarterly session with your leadership team, resolving all key issues, reviewing last quarter's Rocks and setting next quarter's Rocks, getting better and better at it every 90 days. Every year, you participate in a highly effective two-day annual planning session, challenging every aspect of your V/TO and putting a rock-solid plan in place for the coming year, with everyone on the same page.

You're hiring, firing, reviewing, rewarding, and recognizing all of your people around core values and using the People Analyzer for all people decisions. As your organization grows, you're making the necessary evolutionary changes to your Accountability Chart, always focused on structure first and people second, ensuring the right people are in the right seats.

You participate in a weekly Level 10 Meeting with your leadership team, reviewing your Scorecard to assure all numbers are on track. You review Rocks to make sure all priorities are on track. You're solving all relevant issues for the week. As a result, you're executing well as a team. In addition, each department is doing the same.

Every 90 days, you deliver a quarterly state-of-the-company meeting. That keeps everyone in your company on the same page, sharing the same vision. Each person is setting and achieving his or her individual Rocks. Your company is growing. You're achieving your goals and building a great company.

This picture can be achieved. It is just a matter of implementing each tool in the order in which I've laid them out for you in this chapter.

If at any time you get stuck, don't hesitate to reach out to us for help.

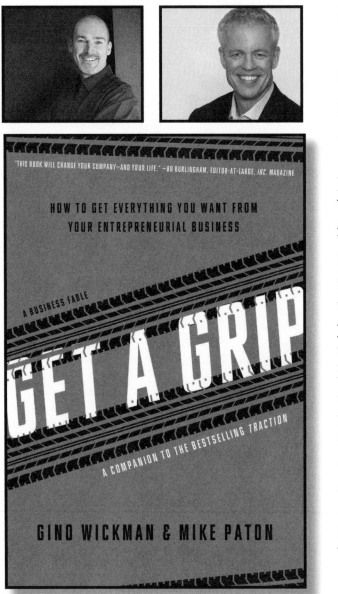

ABOUT THE AUTHOR AND EOS WORLDWIDE

Gino Wickman's passion is helping people get what they want from their businesses. To fulfill that passion, Gino created the Entrepreneurial Operating System (EOS), a holistic system that, when implemented in an organization, helps leaders run better businesses, get better control, have better life balance, and gain more traction; with the entire organization advancing together as a healthy, functional, and cohesive team. Gino spends most of his time as an EOS Implementer, working hands-on with the leadership teams of entrepreneurial companies to help them fully implement EOS in their organizations. He is the founder of EOS Worldwide, a growing organization of successful entrepreneurs from a variety of business backgrounds collaborating as certified EOS Implementers to help people throughout the world to experience all the organizational and personal benefits of implementing EOS. Gino also delivers workshops and keynote addresses.

FOR ADDITIONAL HELP AND INFORMATION

My goal is to help you get everything you want from your business by offering three ways to help you fully and purely implement EOS in your organization:

1. **Self-Implementation**—select one of your most capable and dedicated leaders to teach, facilitate, and coach your leadership team through The EOS Process, using free downloadable tools from our website and this book as a guide;

2. **Supported Self-Implementation**—by joining the EOS Implementer Community for a small monthly fee, we will fully train and support that same leader to become an expert at implementing EOS in your organization; OR

3. **Professional Implementation**—engage a professional EOS Implementer to lead you through The EOS Process.

You can find out more about these three approaches, download free tools, subscribe to our blog for regular helpful tips, find out how to become a professional certified implementer, and schedule speaking engagements at **www.eosworldwide.com**.

If you have any other questions or want any other help, call 1-877-EOS-1877 or e-mail info@eosprocess.com.

Now, an excerpt from

GET A GRIP

By Gino Wickman & Mike Patton

The story of one company's successful implementation
of the EOS system discussed in *Traction*

CHAPTER 1

THE INCIDENT

Sitting in her car, Eileen Sharp stared intently at Vic's SUV parked across the lot. For a brief moment, she envisioned gunning the engine and ramming it. The hint of a smile appeared at the corners of her mouth.

Eileen was angry and frustrated with Vic. For the first time she thought of ending the partnership with her childhood friend. After a few moments, she gathered herself and regained some resolve.

"I'm not walking away from what we've built these last ten years," Eileen said under her breath. "You just don't turn your back on a $7 million company and 35 employees."

Still, what her business partner had done in the meeting was a new low. The fact that he'd said it in front of the other leaders was unforgivable. She couldn't just let it go.

Suddenly Eileen realized she was late for the Business Roundtable reception. She took a deep breath and checked herself in the rearview mirror. As she pulled out of the parking lot she muttered, "That son-of-a-bitch."

Four hours earlier, at 1:00 P.M., Eileen had rushed into the conference room carrying her laptop and a mound of paperwork. Determined to begin Swan Services' quarterly executive committee meeting on time for once, she had scurried around all morning and skipped lunch to prepare the presentation and numerous reports that would tell the "story" of the last 18 months.

This had been the first tough stretch in Swan Services' history. Until the last year and a half, the company had been profitable and had grown quickly. Swan was still doing well, but the steady growth had stopped. Everything seemed to be getting more difficult—winning new customers, keeping them happy, operating profitably—you name it. She had always taken pride in her work ethic, but recently the demands of her business required so much attention that she regularly missed important events with her husband and two children. For the first time Eileen was frustrated, and she could tell that other members of the team were frustrated, too.

Eileen burst through the conference room door, ready to apologize, once again, for being late. Instead, she found only two of her five colleagues. Sue Meecham, Swan's VP of Sales, was reviewing the latest pipeline numbers. Eileen's longtime friend and business associate and the acting Director of Marketing, Art Pearson, was stowing his overcoat and briefcase in the corner of the conference room.

"Hello Sue, hi Art—any sign of the others?" she asked.

"No," replied Sue. "Unless you count Evan racing by a minute ago and looking relieved to see he wasn't the only one late."

Eileen rolled her eyes, dropped her materials at the front of the table, and asked Art to help connect her laptop to the LCD projector. In walked Carol Henning, Swan's Controller. Eileen distributed presentation folders to the three executives and began bringing up the PowerPoint presentation she had prepared. VP of Operations Evan McCullough entered looking rushed and disheveled. And then the team waited.

Vic finally strolled through the door at 1:14, still in the middle of an animated phone conversation with what sounded like a prospective client. He made a few exaggerated gestures to the rest of the team, making it clear he was attempting to end the call. Eventually he hung up, sat down, and apologized as only Vic could.

"Sorry, guys. That was the procurement guy at Shoreline Industries," he said. "I've been trying to pry that deal out of his hands and back under the control of our buyer for so long, I think we used a slide rule to put the bid together."

The entire team laughed—even Eileen. She tossed her founding partner and CEO a folder, strode to the front of the room, grabbed the remote control, and launched into her presentation. Over the next 60 minutes, she detailed the troubling signs that had developed in the five quarters since the company's "breakout year":

- In Swan's eighth full year, revenues grew at a record pace and exceeded $7 million for the first time. However the company hadn't managed to hit its quarterly revenue goals since. Against projected growth of 14 percent, revenue had grown only 1.5 percent in the prior year, and was flat in Q1 this year.

- Profitability had taken a beating. On the heels of a great year, the team had invested heavily in a foundation for further growth. Those investments had not yet paid off.

- Pinpointing the cause of these problems had been difficult. Eileen had been studying the issue for three quarters and now felt comfortable sharing her findings with the team:

  o Swan's sales team had missed its new revenue goal in three of the last five quarters.

  o Existing customers had begun leaving—a new phenomenon. At first the occasional defections seemed trivial, but the trend was disconcerting.

  o Labor costs had increased significantly. Swan had begun adding people and upgrading talent last year in an effort to ramp up to its five-year goal of $20 million in revenue.

  o Despite Swan's paying more for talent, a few key employees had resigned abruptly in recent months. None cited internal issues in exit interviews, but Eileen had come to believe that Swan's once great culture—one devoted to being a genuinely fun place to work hard and get great results—had begun eroding.

None of these issues was new. The team had discussed each one at some length in prior quarterly meetings—often staying late into the night and ordering pizza but rarely reaching agreement on anything, much less a plan of action. The prevailing sense was that the primary cause of all of these issues was somehow outside of their control.

One quarter, the economy was to blame. The next it was the software conversion. Last quarter Vic had actually used the terms "bad mojo" and "funk" in an attempt to quantify the problem—suggesting that the company had lost its "Midas Touch."

"Dwelling on all this bad news drags us down," he had said, staring directly at Eileen. "We've lost our swagger and—while I know some of you will dismiss this as metaphysical mumbo-jumbo—I'm convinced we have to get that swagger back at all cost."

At the time Eileen had taken Vic's observation in stride. She learned long ago to ignore his constant baiting and avoid getting sucked into titanic battles over trivial matters. Instead, Eileen analyzed the situation thoroughly and carefully prepared her plan of attack for today's meeting. She had entered the conference room intent on staying positive and focusing on solutions to the 13 things she believed the executive committee actually *could* control. But first, she needed to present her mountain of evidence to convince them Swan had a right to expect more.

Eileen methodically made her case; the data was irrefutable. Despite a larger budget, Swan's marketing efforts had produced fewer qualified leads. The sales team's close-ratio had declined and it had more frequently offered discounted pricing on the deals it *had* won. In Operations, revenues per employee had fallen while errors and missed deadlines were up.

As she walked through the troubling details, Eileen saw the mood in the conference room change. Arms were uncrossed. Heads began to nod. Notes were taken. Near the end of her presentation, Vic pushed himself away from the conference table and held his hands up dramatically, as though he had eaten too much at Thanksgiving dinner.

"*No mas*, boss," he said with a smile. "We get it."

When the laughter subsided, Eileen suggested the team take a quick break and return ready to start solving problems. In high spirits, she headed for the ladies' room. That's where a nightmare scenario began to unfold.

Eileen heard someone slide quickly into the restroom before the swinging door closed behind her.

"Um, Eileen?"

"Yes, Sue—what is it?" said the startled leader.

"I don't know exactly how to say this," she began. "So I'll just spit it out. I think it would be best for all concerned if I left Swan, effective immediately."

ACKNOWLEDGMENTS

This book would not have been possible without the help and guidance of the following people. I cannot thank them enough for the impact they have had on my life. My heartfelt appreciation goes out to them.

FAMILY AND FRIENDS

Kathy, my strong and beautiful wife, for your love through the good and bad times. Thanks for giving me the freedom to be an entrepreneur and for always believing in me, not to mention the weeks you spent helping me with this book—you were a life saver. I am truly the luckiest husband in the world. I love you.

Alexis, my wise and beautiful daughter, and Gino, my son with the quick wit and common sense—you both keep me humble, make me laugh, and teach me what life is really about. You are the light of my life. You are amazing individuals and the best children a dad could have. I love you both very much.

Linda Wickman, my mom, for teaching me to be independent, for your amazing quiet strength and wisdom, and for always being so proud of me.

Floyd Wickman, my dad and my life mentor. This book would not exist without you. You have taught me everything I know about communicating with people, be it one or one thousand. You exemplify every principle in this book.

Neil Pardun, my father-in-law, for teaching me that it is possible to possess wealth and remain humble. You are a rare and special person. I am forever changed through your example.

Karen Grooms, the greatest assistant on earth. Thanks for holding all of the pieces together and protecting me from distractions so that I may remain in my Unique Ability®. I would be lost without you.

Don Tinney, the best business partner a guy could have and an EOS Implementer extraordinaire. Thank you for proving it is possible that someone other than me can deliver EOS. Your feedback on this book was invaluable.

Mike Pallin, who I truly believe is my guardian angel. You always place in front of me exactly what I need at that point in my life. This book would not have happened without you. I cannot wait to see what you have in store for me next.

The "Book Club," aka Curt Rager and Bob Shenefelt, for being an amazing sounding board and for constantly challenging me. Our annual trip to the mountains gives me tremendous clarity. You are lifers.

Pat Tierney, Rob Tamblyn, and Kevin Brady, my first clients, for letting me practice on you. You gave me the confidence to move forward.

My Entrepreneurs' Organization forum members: John Anderson, Michael Cauley, Dan Dorman, Brian Ferilla, Dan Glisky, Mike Kanan, Scot Lund, Paul Pascoe, Marty Petz, Curt Rager, Bob Shenefelt, and John Silvani, for being an amazing sounding board, great teachers, and my proving ground.

Tyler Smith, for constantly challenging me and not getting caught up in the hype. You are wise beyond your years. Thanks for your guidance and honesty.

Ed Escobar, my previous business partner, for pushing hard and finally convincing my dad to let me into his company. I am on this path because of your belief in me.

John Anderson, one of the world's greatest "connectors," for introducing me to six people who have had a huge impact on my success: Verne Harnish, Pat Lencioni, Dan Sullivan, Craig Erlich, Bill Gitre, and John Gallant. You are one of the most selfless people I know.

MENTORS AND TEACHERS

Sam Cupp, my business mentor, for teaching me all that I know about business. I could not have pulled off that turnaround without your guidance. I hope I have done you proud with this book.

Verne Harnish, for being a pioneer, for inviting me into your world, and showing me that there is a place out there for my craft. Thank you for your passion and the impact you have had on the entrepreneurial world. Your teachings and tools have inspired much of what is in this book.

Pat Lencioni, for your amazing and unparalleled work. I've never met anyone with your combination of humility and talent. You are truly unique. Thank you for your words of wisdom on our drive to the airport. They changed my life.

Dan Sullivan, for helping me discover my Unique Ability® and showing me how to build a life around it. You have made a great impact on my life. You are truly the coach of all coaches.

Jim Collins, for your amazing work, research, and inspiration. Your research on core values, core purpose, putting the right people in the right seats, and proving that "Level 5 Leaders" have a place in the world has simplified my work. You have truly changed the course of business history.

Mr. Sarkisian, Mr. Long, and the late Larry LaFever, for looking at me and treating me as the person I would become when I was a young man. You gave me confidence, and for that I am forever grateful.

CLIENTS AND CONTRIBUTORS

The manuscript readers: Karen Andrews, Thom Barry, Ron Blank, Rob Dube, Dan Israel, Dr. Lawrence Jelsch, Andy Klein, Chris McCuiston, Patrick O'Leary, Curt Rager, Bernie Ronnisch, Todd Sachse, Jim Sheehan, Bob Shenefelt, Tyler Smith, Don Tinney, Tom Violante, David Wallen, and Floyd Wickman. Thanks for all of your valuable time and incredible feedback. You are forever a part of this book.

Gerry Sindell of Thought Leaders International; Ross Slater, Jennifer Tribe, and Susan Hart of Highspot Inc.; and John Paine of John Paine Editorial Services, for helping me find my voice and giving me the direction to write this book.

My clients, for giving me the opportunity to live my dream every day. This book is a by-product of all of our work together, and most of its content comes from you. Thank you for allowing me to use your stories. Without them, this book would not have integrity.

INDEX